Multi-Use Architecture in the Urban Context

MULTI-USE ARCHITECTURE IN THE URBAN CONTEXT

Eberhard H. Zeidler

VNR VAN NOSTRAND REINHOLD COMPANY

New York

Copyright © 1983 by Karl Krämer Verlag,
Stuttgart
Library of Congress Catalog Card Number
83-12496
ISBN 0-442-29388-7

Printed in the United States of America

Published in 1985 by Van Nostrand Reinhold
Company Inc.
135 West 50th Street
New York, New York 10020

Van Nostrand Reinhold Company Limited
Molly Millars Lane
Wokingham, Berkshire RG11 2PY, England

Van Nostrand Reinhold
480 La Trobe Street
Melbourne, Victoria 3000, Australia

Macmillan of Canada
Division of Gage Publishing Limited
164 Commander Boulevard
Agincourt, Ontario M1S 3C7, Canada

16 15 14 13 12 11 10 9 8 7 6 5 4 3 2 1

**Library of Congress Cataloging in
Publication Data**
Zeidler, Eberhard H.
   Multiuse architecture.

   Translation of: Multifunktionale Architek-
tur im städtischen Kontext.
   Bibliography: p. 157
   1. Joint occupancy of buildings—Hand-
books, manuals, etc.   2. City planning—
Handbooks, manuals, etc.
I. Title.
NA4177.Z4513 1984   720
83-12496
ISBN 0-442-29388-7

Contents

Preface

If this book appears to present a number of confusing facts and neither accomplishes to logically organize them into a scientific understanding, nor clarify their emotional substance, then it does only reflect a reality that we have to accept.

As architects we do not have the privilege of either the scientists who can exclude from their realm anything that cannot be scientifically proven, or that of the artist who can ignore the realm of reality and move into a world of emotional expression.

Buildings, and the cities they create, exist in both realms, the one that we can scientifically understand, and the other, that we emotionally respond to. However, such schism exists only in our mind. In reality, an individual building can have only one form, and in fact the act of building is to weld this schism into one expression.

If this lack of exploring neither logical reasoning on one hand, nor poetic expression on the other but instead to happily be muddling in both, is condemned as a shortcoming of this book, then the fault is mine, because against better advice, I pursued this trail.

However, for any merits this book may display, I must give thanks for the tremendous encouragement, impetus and help Professor Jürgen Joedicke has given as the editor, to Paul Cravit for his thankless task of steering me into directions I refused to enter, to Margaret Zeidler, for the extensive research required to assemble the material, to Karl Horst Krämer and Annemarie Bosch for the nearly impossible job of ordering and creating the book, and finally, to my wife Jane, for her never-ending tolerance in sharing with me a life that is consumed with a madness for architecture.

Eberhard H. Zeidler

Introduction

Our most enjoyable cities are those which quietly weave together a rich and complex pattern of different uses and activities. As with any pattern or fabric, these cities need continual care and renewing – the mending and restitching of parts which run down or require change. A fabric of interwoven uses usually evolves over many years, in stages, temporarily reaching periods of economic and social equilibrium, only to change again. Critical to this process is the complementary nature of their uses – how they reinforce each other and how collectively they support everyday life.

Regrettably, the pioneers of modern architecture did not consider interconnectedness within a city to be important. Instead they viewed cities as containers for many separate functions, each one suffocating the others unless they were kept separated. Although today's cities suffer from problems similar to those addressed by early modern architects, time has changed our viewpoints and consequently our analyses of these problems. We are not so ready today to see our cities as malfunctioning bodies requiring surgery, especially the radical surgery too often prescribed in the past, but recognize in their apparent confusion their inherent vitality.

Many people have contributed to this changing analysis of our cities, among them social thinkers, architects, planners and politicians; but particularly influential were the complaints of those who have had to live in the misconceptions of modern planning. Failure of such Utopian models as urban renewal, satellite suburbs, office campuses and the like has demonstrated the insensitivity – and futility – of a modern planning philosophy which ignored the interdependence of everyday activities. Today, however, the relationship of a building's activities with its surroundings again concerns most architects working in the urban context.

This book looks at a particular aspect of urban architecture – buildings or groups of buildings which fulfill multiple uses – and focuses on their urban implications. Since the multi-use building is a function of its environment, it would not exist without the city that nurtures it. Therefore, we must not only examine multi-use structures in isolation but also within the context of the cities that give rise to them. Some questions investigated are:

Do such buildings make both physical connection and social reference to their surroundings?

Do they encourage pedestrian use of the street and yet facilitate traffic movement?

Do they provide public amenities and a better use of urban space?

Do they create a framework that supports different uses to their common benefit?

Simply put, do multi-use buildings enrich the city's fabric? I think they can do so.

Yet multi-use buildings are not a placebo for urban problems. There are no guarantees that in certain situations a multi-use project would serve any better than single-use buildings. Even today too many massive multi-use complexes have been built with the same sweeping urban renewal intent witnessed in the 1950's . . . only that they are now intended for the consumer. Too often they have swallowed up the varied uses and activities along the street and sealed them into a monotonous indoor environment. However, many successful projects exist that are more sensitive to their urban situations: the Stuttgart Redevelopment Project, Toronto's St. Lawrence neighbourhood and the Utrecht Music Centre, to name a few.

The multi-use building discussed in this book is an idea, a concept rather than a narrowly defined building form. It includes all buildings that harbour more than one of the three main functions of human life. Not only should the multi-use building integrate these internal functions, but it should also relate them to a greater, external urban context.

Therefore a relatively small building which acts as a link in an urban space and a large complex that is almost a city district in itself can both be multi-use structures.

The concept of multi-use is full of unexplored complexities, at least partly because modern architectural theories had denied it to us.

This building type embodies the memory of past urban life, vestiges of which still survive in our cities, and gives us hope for a new, better urban environment.

The multi-use building promises to resurrect from the failures of the past and the confusing complexity of the present a building form that allows urban life again to unfold. Fulfilling the needs of urban life is no longer seen as requiring segregation of its elements, but as demanding a fusion between them. The projects illustrated in Part II include a very divergent group of buildings which have only one thing in common: *Multi-use.*

Portmann's Renaissance Centre has a magnitude of scale that seems to be necessary to re-introduce multi-use into a decayed American downtown, even if we must admit failure of this complex to integrate into its urban fabric.

Hopefully, however, such complexes started an evolutionary trend of accepting multi-use in the downtown that will again permit the smaller scale building to enter the urban scene.

Both the historic precedents and the immediate modern past must be seen in a new perspective, the best of both should be considered. We must abandon our pretence that our own creativeness springs from our imagination uninfluenced by what has happened before.

Neither should our future exclude the concepts created during the half century that modern architecture held sway; nor should romantic delusion make the memory of the past the predominant rule.

The book then is written in this spirit: to examine what is there and to see how we can achieve a better environment through the integration of the multi-use building in the urban fabric.

The book is divided into three parts. Part I discusses some important precedents of multi-use buildings. It also underlines the critical circumstances which led to the abandonment of multi-use buildings as a viable urban model. Part II presents, *without comment,* the plans and photographs of various multi-use projects from different countries. They represent many approaches, from small-scale rehabilitation schemes to larger downtown complexes. To omit any comment, praise or criticism was done deliberately. It is too easy to use a building in its photographic reproduction as an isolated example to prove a particular point. Such action is often unfair to the building when considered in its total complexity and serves little purpose other than to prove the brilliance of the critic. Life, and the reality of Architecture within it, is much more complex and its comprehension is much more demanding. I believe, however, that the conclusions will become selfevident in studying these examples. Part III considers the concept of the multi-use building in terms of its problems and potential urban benefits. By discussing these principles here independently it is my hope that they may be used in studying the examples exhibited in Part II. I consider this a more positive attitude towards a better understanding of our task to rehabilitate our urban environment. In this sense the book is an Architectural Cookbook and I don't consider this as a derogatory comment, because cookbooks are essential. They not only show the finished product, but they also instruct us how to achieve that product; and if it is a good cookbook, it will also discuss the ingredients and their affinity, which then allows another creative cook to consider new variations. For this reason a cookbook is of interest to the cook and only indirectly to the dinner guest.

Part I
Historical Precedents
of Multi-Use Buildings

Before the industrial revolution, describing buildings as multi-use would have seemed irrelevant. Such buildings existed as a matter of course and were integrated into the fabric of European towns and cities. They have been built and used by man for centuries.

The Greek Agora and Roman Baths are well-known examples of early multi-use structures. The Agora, the secular centre of the Greek city, was more than just an orderly arrangement of market stalls. The space around it served as the social and political forum for citizens where gatherings and discussions of all kinds took place. The Baths, too, were centres for public discussion, not merely places for exercise and entertainment. They contained in formal, usually symmetrical plan, a great variety of uses and activities: libraries, theatres, lecture halls, sports rooms and dining facilities.

In Roman and Greek society work was considered neither full-time nor all-consuming, and the importance attributed to public life – to being a citizen – was symbolized both physically and emotionally in their multi-use public buildings. Such structures reflected the spirit and form of the societies which fashioned them.

Civic multi-use buildings were less important in societies that valued a religious or commercial life above a public one. Medieval cities offer a case in point. Here the functions of the large multi-use civic buildings characteristic of Roman and Greek society were fulfilled by smaller private buildings. For example, as Howard Saalman describes in his book, "Medieval Cities", the earliest town councils were held 'not in a structure specifically created for this purpose but in private buildings, generally semi-fortified towers'.

The walls of medieval towns enclosed all activities of an inhabitant's life. With the exception of a few isolated functions served by Church or city hall, his daily activities were circumscribed and contained within his own house. Burghers usually lived above the shops in which they worked. Residence and work place coexisted within one structure, creating the most enduring multi-use building of any city, old or new. Such private multi-use buildings characterized the medieval town and contributed to its distinct form.

Medieval cities eventually became congested with too many buildings inside their walls. Little space remained for the more successful to erect new and larger homes, so they moved outside the walls. Thus, as Saalman notes, "Residence and shop, production and consumption, became separate. The bourgeoise became a commuter." The split had been made, foreshadowing today's surburban dormitories.

In the compact, comparatively immobile society of the Middle Ages, the street was the place of business. It made perfect sense to work beside, in or above it. But the social arrangement of medieval cities changed, and so too did the use of their buildings. In Renaissance and Baroque cities, housing was still frequently situated over street-level shops; however, neither the owner nor the worker in the shop below necessarily lived there.

Even before the industrial revolution the one-to-one relationship of work place to residence, common in medieval times, had become more difficult and less practical to achieve. Because of increasing populations and greater concentration within cities, it became necessary to stack many residences over a single place of work.

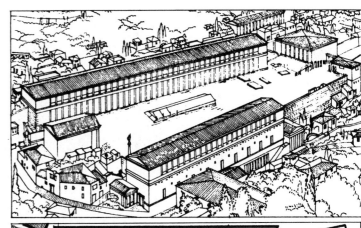

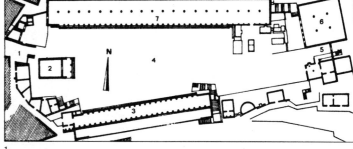

1
The Greek Agora

2
Town wall of Rothenburg enclosing
the activities of the medieval burgher

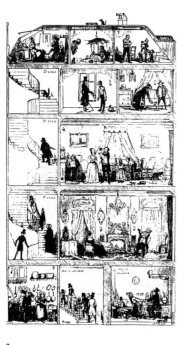

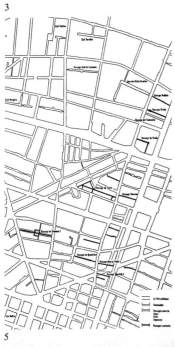

3

5

4

6

7

The Parisian walk-up apartment block of the early 1800's is a well known example of this. The ground level was given over to shops, restaurants, cafés and theatres. Above them were four or five floors of apartments. Elegant versions of this model, such as those along the Rue de Rivoli, had a continuous arcade at ground level which protected the shopper and visually unified the street elevation. Haussmann adopted this model as the basic building block for his highly successful streets and boulevards.

One of the more remarkable developments of this multi-use commercial/ residential model was the enclosed passage or galleria. A horizontal collection of these apartment blocks formed one long, continuous, double-sided pedestrian mall covered by a glass roof but open at each end to the street. Such passages emerged as a viable building type in Europe at the same time as the Parisian walk-up apartments; they spread with equal appeal as an urban model to North America.

Passages can be knit into the city fabric, incorporating existing buildings into their overall structure. However, the extraordinary urban potential of enclosed galleries has been best illustrated in Paris. Here a complex network of passages was built around Boulevard Montmartre, exploiting the narrow, deep Parisian lots between streets, breathing new life into the middle of these blocks and opening new pedestrian walks.

Apart from their obvious urban benefits they were practical from a real estate viewpoint too, consuming little expensive frontage because of their perpendicular positioning to the street. Such structures were extremely lucrative largely because of the matrix of uses they contained. Shops, light industrial establishments, nightclubs, restaurants, cafés, and even museums were accommodated on the ground floor. Apartments, sometimes converted to office spaces, occupied the floors above.

In plan, they usually employed a regular column grid adjusted according to site constraints. Each bay had its own private stair; occasional public stairs serviced such uses as second-floor restaurants. Apartments, generally two stories high, had their parlours facing onto the mall and the more private spaces, like bedrooms, were above the glass roof. Despite the many variations to the basic passage model, all maintained a similar vertical division of uses.

Though passages spread rapidly in popularity during the nineteenth century and often employed the latest advances in steel and glass technology, in the minds of modern historians they remained somewhat removed from the spirit of the industrial age. Despite their often grand size and elegant appeal, they were too modest an invention, too closely connected to the existing city fabric to characterize a break with the past. That distinction would be left to huge exhibition halls, railway stations and heroic engineering works. Separated from the reality of city life by space, standing proudly alone, such herculean projects proclaimed the achievements of the industrial revolution.

The significance of passages rested elsewhere. They represented the rich potential of adding to and renewing the existing city on a human scale. They did not attempt to reinvent parts of the city, nor do away with it in a clean sweep. The problems they addressed were limited to their immediate urban context, yet they demonstrated a larger possibility for the city as a whole – the idea of continuous and active pedestrian networks.

Today the passages that survive in Paris and other cities are still as active and alive as they were when first constructed. They exist as one of the last and best examples of a truly urban multi-use structure.

Industrialism and Utopias: The End of Multi-Use Buildings

The industrial revolution dramatically changed the shape of cities. Previous ways of building and thinking about them seemed obsolete. As long as cities remained relatively stable commercial and administrative centres, their intricate physical fabric could be understood as a natural consequence of these activities. However, the industrial revolution brought with it a whole range of new uses and activities which were difficult to incorporate into the existing fabric. The scale of urban problems became magnified and seemingly unmanageable. Simple reforms would not do.

The type of work most people did was completely and permanently changed by the machine revolution. Cottage industries carried out at home by individual families were no longer economically viable. To make a living, people had to use machines. This meant working in the new factories, factories which were in the heart of cities. So the newly built railroads linking country to city brought a sudden influx of people to industrialized cities, resulting in dramatically acceler-

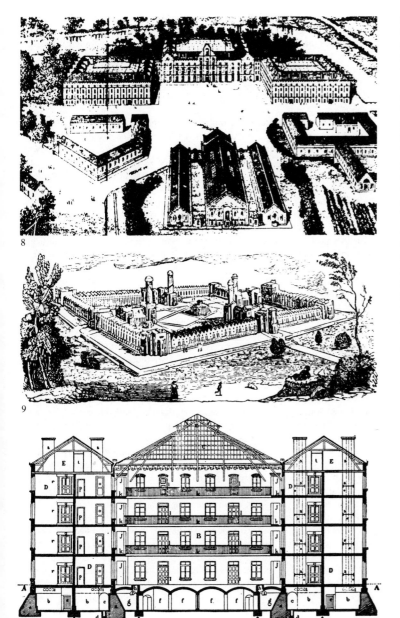

8

9

10

ated urban growth. London of 1800 had about a million residents. In just over thirty years that population doubled. Throughout all industrialized countries such statistics were equally staggering. In America, the urban population rose from less than half a million to over five million in the forty years from 1830 to 1870.

Not only had society's fundamental structure changed, so too had living conditions. Benevelo describes this situation in his "The Origins of Modern Town Planning:" "Residential quarters naturally tended to be built near the place of work, so that houses and factories were often in close contact, intermingled at random and mutually inconvenient. Factory smoke permeated the houses and factory waste polluted the water, while industrial movement was generally hopelessly impeded by private traffic." "The chaos was constantly aggravated by the dynamic nature of the factories involved. Factories were transformed and expanded, houses were demolished and rebuilt, the outskirts of cities crept further into the countryside without ever finding a definite balance."

American and European cities faced similar social problems aggravated by industrialization: poverty, illiteracy, crime, alcoholism, prostitution and insanity. It is therefore no wonder social critics regarded cities as physically and morally decaying environments. Inevitably, proposals were made to establish idealized communities based on alternatives to the capitalism considered to be instrumental in creating the various urban problems. The Utopians wanted more than piece-meal remedial legislation aimed at improving health and sanitary conditions. They demanded that a whole new society be built.

Men such as Robert Owen, Charles Fourier and Saint Simon proposed communities based on a still infant and naive form of socialism. They established rules for their communities, rules that governed everything from broad social issues such as property ownership, to more particular building and planning details such as road widths and tree planting. Their work, spanning the end of the 18th and the beginning of the 19th centuries, formed the initial seeds of modern town planning philosophy. This philosophy would strongly influence the CIAM's thinking about their doctrine for a functional city, a doctrine which interrupted the rich history of multi-use urban buildings.

Three main ideas emerged from the Utopian movement which facilitated the shift from traditional town building ideas to a completely new set of principles. First, the ideal Utopian community was an isolated entity located within a benign and receptive landscape, free from the chaos of city life. Since the city with all its conflicting uses and resultant social injustices was viewed as the enemy, the Utopians conveniently removed their solutions for it from the battleground.

Godin's Familistere illustrates this ambition: "Since there is no building facing the Familistere there are no curious neighbours to peer from their windows. On a fine summer evening each inhabitant has only to close the door opening on the great hall to be able to sit at the open window and smoke his pipe or read his book in complete privacy, for all the world as if he were the owner of a *separate* (emphasis mine) villa standing in its own grounds."

Secondly, Utopian communities were restricted to a certain size and number of inhabitants. The ideal city was not to be a limitless container for people and activities. The sheer weight of human numbers present in industrialized cities not only irrevocably changed the pattern of city life, but created a multitude of social ills that the Utopians wished to avoid. It is no coincidence that later Utopian schemes by modern architects like Le Corbusier placed similar emphasis on an ideal size. It was argued that if a community could be restricted to a reasonable size, it would then be socially and physically manageable. Unfortunately, this idealized viewpoint avoided the reality of expanding industrial cities.

Thirdly, Utopians proposed a zoning of uses as a way of reducing social problems. Communities were studied, then their parts sorted out, segregated, and arranged into plans so that potential conflicts could be avoided. There were ironies in some applications of this concept. Though Charles Fourier's Phalanstery building combined various activities in what was clearly a multi-use structure, it was carefully designed to segregate them, as the following shows: "One of the wings ought to combine all noisy workshops such as the carpenter's shop, the forge and all hammer work. It ought also to contain all the industrial gatherings of children who are generally very noisy in industry. The other wing ought to contain the caravansary with its ballrooms and its halls appropriate to intercourse with outsiders so that these may not encumber the central portion of the palace and embarrass the domestric relations."

3
Section of Parisian walk-up apartment

4
Elevation, Parisian walk-up

5
City plan of Paris, showing blocks and passages

6
Cleveland Mall

7
Paris Passage

8
St. Simon

9
Robert Owen

10
Godin, Familistere Section

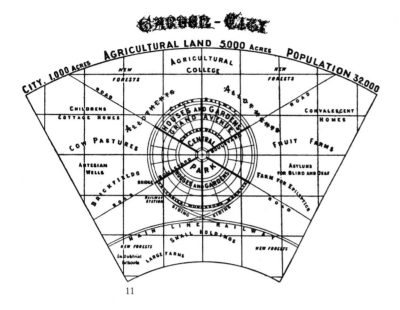

11

12

Yesterday

Living and Working in the Smoke

To-day

Living in the Suburbs – Working in the Smoke

To-morrow

Living & Working in the Sun at WELWYN GARDEN CITY

The work of Utopians influenced other urban concepts being developed at the same time in America and Europe. These various philosophical developments combined with Utopian principles and formed an ideological base for modern town planning doctrines – doctrines which denied the value of the multi-use structure as a significant urban model. To understand the disfavour and subsequent disappearance of multi-use buildings in modern times, it is necessary to explain the philosophical milieu in which this development took place.

The ideas of the radical English philosopher and Utopiast, Jeremy Bentham, were sympathetically received in America in the early years of the 19th century. Both America and Europe faced similar urban problems caused by growing industrialization, and both were searching for ways to solve them. Yet the fundamental underpinnings of American society were quite different. America had matured with the values of an agrarian-based tradition which connected moral character to rural life. Thomas Jefferson, philosopher, architect and statesman, who personified this tradition had frequently warned about the evils of city life. Bentham's Utilitarian movement provided American social thinkers with the most convincing argument for reshaping that tradition into an urban philosophy suiting the American character. Bentham and Jefferson argued for a rational, scientific approach to democratic government. Both believed the only acceptable morality was to attain the greatest good for the greatest number. Accordingly, those subscribing to their views who wished to correct urban evils sought to improve such indices as sanitary conditions, health standards, fresh air, open space, and recreational and educational facilities.

There was a strong connection between the English and American Park Movements which originated during this period and from this philosophy. Parks and accessibility to schooling for all, previously the privilege of the wealthy, were seen as almost moral saviours of society's ills.

Frederick Law Olmsted, the most influential American park designer of the 19th century, incorporated the Utilitarian philosophy in park plans for a number of American cities. His designs were later expanded into complete park systems. Landscaped space, symbolic of a more leisurely and healthful society, was being put back into cities.

The Utopiasts had proposed ideal manageable communities away from the city; the Park Movement had advocated a particular tool for regenerating the city itself – both had given further fuel to the concept of segregation of uses. The belief that moral and social worth could be attached to the park lent credence to its value as part of an emerging urban planning philosophy.

By the time Ebenezer Howard's Garden City project was published in 1898 the ideas behind it had already been articulated, debated and accepted as the proper direction for planning new cities. His project was based on theories of a co-operative society similar to those developed by the Utopiasts.

The Garden City radiated outward in concentric circles from a commercial and cultural centre to a greenbelt of agricultural land. Civic buildings stood alone in the centre on individual grounds. Industry, housing and schools were given their own separate preserves. Size and population were regulated, the maximum held at thirty thousand people.

Jane Jacobs articulated the significance of Howard's plan in her book, "The Death and Life of Great American Cities": "Howard set spinning powerful and city-destroying ideas. He conceived that the way to deal with the city's functions was to sort out of the whole certain simple uses and to arrange each of these in relative self-containment."

Such a planning philosophy had no need for multi-use buildings. Indeed, the multi-use structure was considered part of the city's general confusion, confusion which must be eliminated or minimized. It was hardly a building model which the modern movement architects could embrace.

To all intents and purposes the idea of existing cities being viable and dynamic social habitats had been totally abandoned by the beginning of the 20th century. People were not searching out ways to renew cities, for which multi-use buildings would have been valuable; instead they wanted to make new cities that replaced the old.

In retrospect, it would be as unfair as it is popular to characterize the modern architects who translated this philosophy into buildings as villains in a kind of urban conspiracy. Projects such as Le Corbusier's Ville Radieuse, a particularly influential one, should be viewed in the context of his complete work. It was a powerful and in many ways poetic statement of the more humane society he envisaged. Unfortunately, his society required a "new man" to inhabit it – something which would not happen. But more importantly, its creation required the systematic disassembling of the existing city – something which could not be allowed to happen.

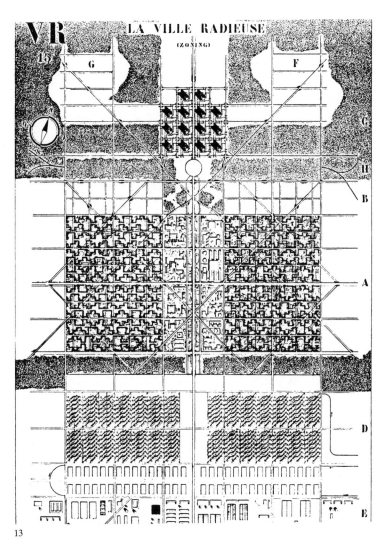

LA VILLE RADIEUSE
(ZONING)

13

Most of these schemes were also extremely naive about the political structure that could realize them. The dream of a communal society that acts through acquiescence towards such fixed goals could ultimately only end up in a dictatorial system as Karl Popper has pointed out.

CIAM and The Supremacy of the Functional City

The Congress International Architecture Moderne (CIAM) was formed in 1928 in Sarraz, Switzerland, following the pathetic results of the League of Nations' Competition. The hoped for formal recognition of a new era of architecture and town planning had disintegrated into a petty squabble between judges, masking the real differences in ideological positions.

Spurred by this failure, architects took matters into their own hands and organized an international meeting of minds. It was an extraordinary beginning. For the first time ever, leading architects from around the world came together at Sarraz to chart a new course for architecture and city planning.

The critical work of CIAM was produced at their fourth meeting in August, 1933. The participants had prepared their homework well. Thirty-three cities were discussed and analyzed, and out of this emerged a statement of principles, the Athens Charter. In it, CIAM architects recognized some of the limitations of the Garden City concept: "Since the advent of the garden cities, a generous movement launched by the English to release men from the inhumanity of the modern city, municipal officials tend to regard the single family house as the sole remedy for a disastrous situation. Unhappily this solution leads to a scattering of dwellings and to the complete alienation of certain inhabited areas. Now the aim is not the dissemination of the elements of the city, but rather . . . the aeration of the city."

In other words, the single family house was a rural, land-consuming concept that was not applicable to cities. Apartments would serve better, freeing the ground for enjoyment.

"The aeration of the city" was a particulary telling phrase. It implied, despite their disclaiming of non-dissemination of a city's elements, a rather complete overhaul of the city. In practice, the Charter advocated the dispersion and segregation of a city's parts.

Both the enthusiastic language of the Athens Charter and its unabashed self-righteousness presented an extremely compelling case. In ninety-five carefully worded clauses the Charter dissected the problems of the city and proposed quite precisely what to do about them. "The Athens Charter *unlocks all doors* to the urbanism of modern times. It is a reply to the present chaos of cities. In the hands of the authorities, itemized, annotated, clarified with an adequate explanation, the Athens Charter is the implement by which *the destiny of cities will be set right.*" (both emphases mine)

Four urban functions were listed: inhabiting, working, recreation (in leisure time), and circulation. Having thus identified these functions, the Charter went on to explain their value in city planning terms: "The four key functions of urbanism have called for special measures offering each function the conditions most favourable to the development of its own activity so that they may . . . bring order and classification to the usual conditions of life, work and culture . . . Each key function will have its own autonomy . . . each will be regarded as an entity to which land and buildings will be allocated, and all of the prodigious resources of modern techniques will be used in arranging and equipping them."

The Athens Charter formalized the modern architectural movement's city planning philosophy into a programme for building. It remained more or less intact over the next 25 years, reinforced by the works of leading architects. Sigfried Giedion, perhaps best of any, expressed prevailing architectural thought in his book, "Space, Time and Architecure": "In earlier times the association of production with dwelling quarters was quite natural, but this connection could not be carried over into large towns . . . If in an industrial age the various functions of daily life cannot be clearly separated, that fact alone spells the death sentence of the great city."

Other books told the same story. The imagery employed recalled earlier descriptions of the "cancerous and sick" industrial cities. Le Corbusier's "Looking at City Planning" spoke of "the street with its ruckus and mechanized terror, the mortal enemy of children". Sert, in his forbiddingly titled book, "Can Our Cities be Saved?", echoed a similar sentiment about the traditional street. He even went so far as to explain the military advantages (in case our cities are bombed) to be gained by the highrise versus the complex city fabric approach.

If cities were indeed cruel puzzles which need total rearranging, then perhaps only the orderly approach prescribed by the CIAM could save it. But some

15

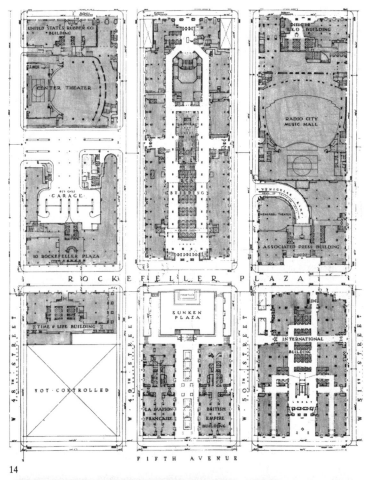

14

15

16

doubted this. Other approaches were made. One in particular is significant for its originality and disregard of the Athens Charter – New York's Rockefeller Centre.

The Rockefeller Centre: Renewing the Old City

In the midst of the depression, at the same time as the Athens Charter was drafted, a major development project was being designed in New York – The Rockefeller Centre. It represented an important departure in city planning, especially for one of the apparently diseased cities discussed at Athens. It pointed in another, older direction, one re-scaled to the modern city. Heroic in size, it stands in the middle of Manhattan, a vital part of the city's tremendous life. By any definition it is a multi-use project, contrary to the modern movement's doctrine of segregated functions.

If we leave aside its obvious architectural delights and look only at the street level plan, we see a scheme that respects the traditional street pattern. It creates an imaginative, active public space – the sunken plaza – in its centre. Below street level, a shopping concourse connects the various buildings of the complex in a pedestrian system tied into the subway. Access to the public plaza can be gained from this level as well. Yet the treatment of ground level, its approach to the traditional New York Street, contributes greatly to its success and distinguishes it from the then current functionalist planning philosophy.

The sunken plaza is a rather extraordinary piece of urban topography – a lush valley inside the dry, flat New York grid. The juxtaposition of this festive public space with its hard urban surroundings gives it an oasis-like appeal. Compare this to pristine office districts amidst endless green, or to temple-like towers on wind-swept plazas.

The complete project, down to its smallest and most gracious detail, demonstrates the value attached to everyday events in the city. Tired shoppers rest by fountains leading to the plaza, office workers sun themselves on the many roof gardens, elegant and not-so-elegant café habitués enjoy the surroundings – all are part of the story which has been considered and quietly accommodated.

The architects at Athens, and many still today, would argue for more space around the building. Bylaws enacted in American cities demand today that buildings be set back. Yet the Rockefeller Centre buildings touch on the street and do so successfully, maintaining the street's façade. Its towers are stepped back to allow sunshine in, for its designers also gave attention to the sky, the street, and the pedestrian.

According to the modern building philosophy, theatres would have been set back from the street – for symbolic as well as practical reasons – spill-over room for performance times. However, the crowds lining the sidewalks alongside the Centre's Radio City Music Hall are as much an event as the long-legged chorus girls inside. The Centre went against modern theory and created a vibrant, lively people place; in contrast, witness all the dead cultural centres surrounded by parking lots that bear witness to the segregated approach.

The Rockefeller Centre represented a spirited attack on the planning ideals of the Athens Charter. Like the enclosed passages and gallerias, it suggested possibilities for existing cities in large-scale multi-use projects. It demonstrated the interconnectedness of city life, the mutual dependence of different uses, and the improved urban fabric which can be achieved by recognizing this interdependence.

14
Rockefeller Centre
Street level plan

15
Rockefeller Centre
Sunken plaza. Skillful combination of urban space and urban activities

16
Rockefeller Centre
Concourse level

17
Rockefeller Centre
Design respects traditional street pattern

18
Patterns of association

17

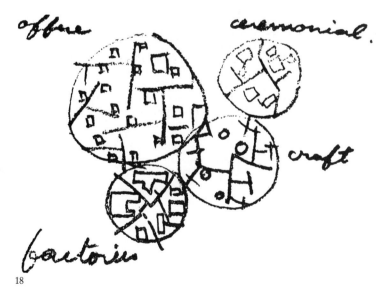

18

After Otterlo – The Renewal of Multi-Use Buildings

By the end of the 1950's, ideological changes had developed within CIAM's ranks. The functional city proclaimed in words and works during the preceding decades had not worked. Despite some stunning examples of excellent individual buildings, cities themselves had not been transformed into the more liveable and humane habitats initially envisioned. On the contrary, many urban problems such as social communications and urban congestion which CIAM architects attempted to rectify had been aggravated.

The failure in CIAM thinking lay in basic shortsightedness. They saw only what was convenient and supportive of their new manifesto. Aldo Van Eyck said it best during the CIAM meeting at Otterlo in 1958: "What is really wrong stems from the other enemy – the enemy of a system of analysis of 'city' – a creation of four keys, keys which don't fit the lock. We know because the lock never opened, the system never opened the lock to the human heart. This was a system, a system which may have been important at one time in order to canalize – canalize all the objections and the terrible results of chaotic cities in the 19th century. But it made an absolute. It made an absolute out of traffic and an absolute out of housing and an absolute out of reaction. But it understood nothing of what these things were really about."

The Otterlo meeting was a historic turning point. A younger generation of architects led by Van Eyck and other Team 10 members rejected the picture of the city painted by the Athens Charter. Instead they turned to existing cities and the complex network of social relationships within them. By re-examining how people actually lived the Team 10 architects confirmed the invalidity of the old CIAM approach and began forming more realistic planning models.

Of particular importance to the new analysis was the work of Peter and Allison Smithson. Their studies in patterns of association resulted in systems of linked buildings which were intended to correspond closely with the actual network of social relationships. Such linked building systems were counter to the CIAM's doctrine of finite spaces and self-contained buildings. As the Smithsons explained: "This conception is in direct opposition to the arbitrary isolation of the so-called communities of the Unité and the neighbourhood. We are of the opinion that such a hierarchy of human associations should replace the functional hierarchy of the Charte d'Athens."

The street, attacked by the moderns and eliminated or reduced to interior circulations, was resurrected by Team 10 in new ways, such as the elevated streets that as decked walkways connected housing blocks, still curiously Untité-like in appearance. The same principle was applied to their Sheffield University Extension scheme using a connecting circulation spine.

Yet even though their buildings were linked, they still only catered to single uses, and like the CIAM projects they criticized, their ground plans remained devoted to flowing green spaces. The pedestrian street in the air was to replace the one on the ground – and yet it is the street on the ground that moulds a city's form. Team 10 architects had not fully embraced the physical form and dimensions of the old city. As pointed out by the magazine, "Architectural Design": "It was somehow not right to rebuild the old pattern. If one considers movement as the mainspring of urban building, more radical forms come into being."

Team 10 projects did not rebuild the old pattern. Yet by developing a vocabulary of connection for their concepts – link, web, stem and spine – by emphasizing the idea of connection, they suggested a new way of building within the old pattern. Their concepts recognized the implications of a mobile society in the same way the Athens Charter had addressed the spirit of an industrialized society. Increased mobility implied increased change. Buildings were seen not as finite, fixed in programme and junction, but rather as generous, adaptable frameworks for a variety of conditions and uses.

The Berlin Free University project by Candilis, Josic and Woods gave impetus to this idea. As these architects explained: "The question is not to build flexible buildings but to establish an environment in which buildings appropriate to their function may occur, and to encourage an interaction between these buildings and their environment."

This was getting closer to the concept of multi-use. In a sense the Free University project almost brought the urban building full circle. It restored the pedestrian street to its former importance and created buildings which could support a variety of uses commensurate with social needs and physical demands.

The project introduced a new, totally urban concept: the mat building. In it only traffic and structural grids were established. It lacked the internal segregation and the formal expression of different functions – both ideas sacred to modern architecture.

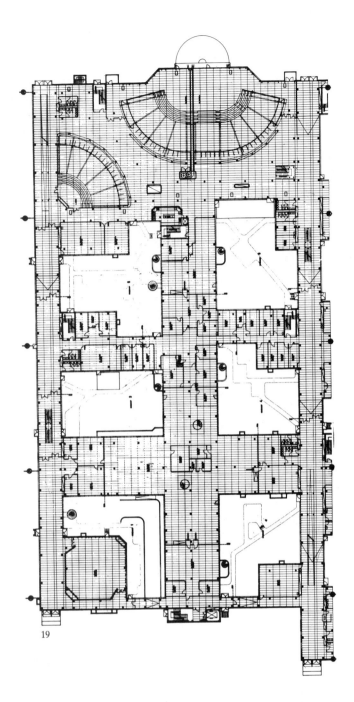

19

The scheme in effect was a mini-town. Yet the mat building was still a child of the modern movement and related to the megastructure that envisaged the city as a single building.

Reyner Banham defined the megastructure as: "On one hand a massive, even monumental, supporting frame; on the other, various arrangements of habitable containers beyond the control of the architect."

However, the development of the mat concept created a flexible building that could accept different and changing uses. It rejected the rigid single use of earlier modern models, but also the monumental form of the megastructure. The mat building was indeterminable and capable of adhering to different urban fabric. Thus, the mat building can serve as a point of departure from our discussion of historical background.

However, the multi-use building moves beyond the confining concept of the megastructure, for it accepts again the fabric of the city as the spiritual framework and sees itself as a link within such context.

It is important to realize the consequences of such a concept. On the surface it may appear as if such action would be retrogressive and deny us a vision of a splendid future: totally different – the brave new world, Archigram, Star wars – the heroic future projected into the galaxies.

Paolo Soleri and his Arcology is still seen by the public as a possible solution of this dream, as witnessed by the many that are drawn to his experiment. Yet even if it would be technically possible and economically feasible to create such Super Sculptural Architecture in its full romanticism, what political system would be required to force individuals into such unalterable confinement? One does not have to quote Popper and his theories on Utopia to recognize the consequences for the individual. Compared to this, the Ville Radieuse was a mere embryonic stutter of such new city. Arcology will never be a new direction, but is a final, even if beautiful, calcification of a species of urban dynosaurs.

The acceptance of the rejected traditional city framework, on the contrary, is not retrogressive, but opens up again an urban life based on individual freedom within a democratic political structure. We should not let the similarity of the resulting urban form with those of the past confuse us not to recognize its different character.

It will not do just to apply historic precedents to find the solution. Regardless of how enticing the recreation of Vienna Gründerstil may be to us as expressed in the vision of the brothers Krier; such simplification could be as poisonous a tonic to the urban life as Soleri's galactic visions.

While the new urban space is still articulated by a syntax that uses streets and squares for its expression, the elements that will form them are different. We cannot overlook that we live in a post-industrial world, that we expect freedom of opportunity, of movement and of comfort that were not available for all in the city of the past. Our ability to create such conditions depends on the efficiency that we create in our built environment, and in this sense the Moderns were right.

But it also depends on the emotional response that the built environment evokes in us. It is the acceptance of this contradiction within the urban environment that opens the way into the future.

The multi-use building must not only respond to the functional needs of our time, but also to the urban fabric and its emotional and political presence.

It is in the hope that the multi-use building may broaden our vocabulary to create such urban language that I want to discuss its potential as such an urban building block.

20

19
Candilis, Josic, Woods, Schiedhelm
Berlin Free University

20
Candilis, Josic, Woods, Schiedhelm
Freie Universität Berlin
Still a megastructure that remains a single building isolated from the context of the surrounding city

Part II
The Projects

19

Affleck, Desbarats, Dimakopoulos, Lebensold, Sise: Place Bonaventure, Montreal, CDN, 1967

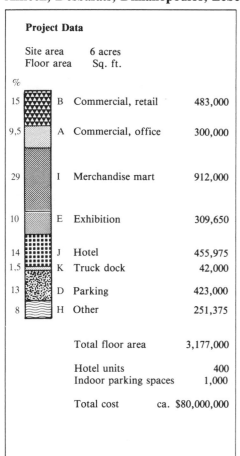

Project Data

Site area	6 acres		
Floor area	Sq. ft.		

%				Sq. ft.
15	B	Commercial, retail		483,000
9,5	A	Commercial, office		300,000
29	I	Merchandise mart		912,000
10	E	Exhibition		309,650
14	J	Hotel		455,975
1,5	K	Truck dock		42,000
13	D	Parking		423,000
8	H	Other		251,375
		Total floor area		3,177,000
		Hotel units		400
		Indoor parking spaces		1,000
		Total cost	ca.	$80,000,000

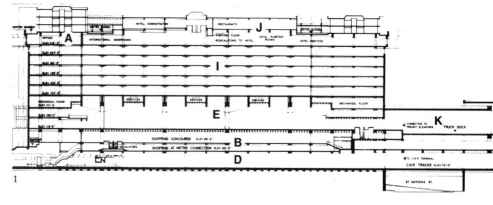

1

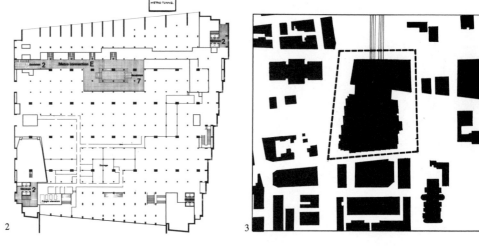

2
3

1 Cross section looking East
2 Plan of lower shopping level and metro connection
3 Figure ground plan
4 Ground floor-shopping concourse plan
5 Elevation
6 Aerial view
7 View of hotel roof garden
8 View of hotel lobby
9 View of hotel roof garden

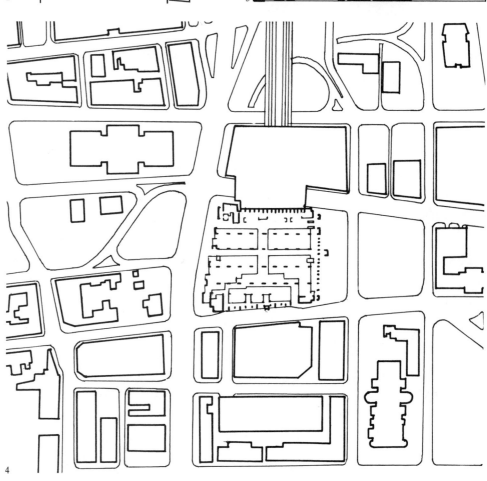

4

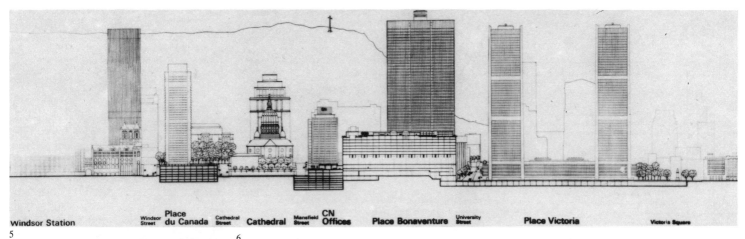

Windsor Station   Windsor Street   **Place du Canada**   Cathedral Street   **Cathedral**   Mansfield Street   **CN Offices**   **Place Bonaventure**   University Street   **Place Victoria**   Victoria Square

5

6

7

8

9

James A. Murray + Henry Fliess: The Towne, Toronto, CDN, 1967

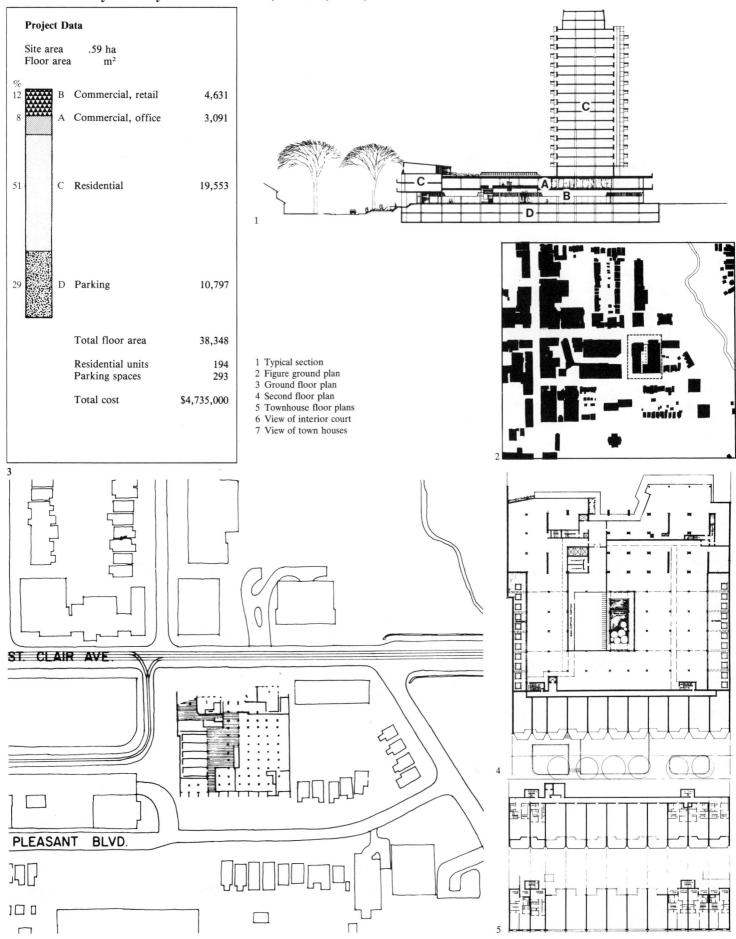

Project Data

Site area	.59 ha		
Floor area	m²		

%				
12	B	Commercial, retail	4,631
8	A	Commercial, office	3,091
51	C	Residential	19,553
29	D	Parking	10,797

Total floor area	38,348
Residential units	194
Parking spaces	293
Total cost	$4,735,000

1 Typical section
2 Figure ground plan
3 Ground floor plan
4 Second floor plan
5 Townhouse floor plans
6 View of interior court
7 View of town houses

ST. CLAIR AVE.

PLEASANT BLVD.

J. von Gagern: Amalienpassage, München, D, 1968–1973 · 1979–1980

Project Data

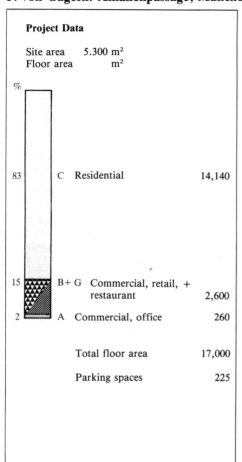

Site area	5.300 m²		
Floor area	m²		

%			
83	C	Residential	14,140
15	B+ G	Commercial, retail, + restaurant	2,600
2	A	Commercial, office	260
		Total floor area	17,000
		Parking spaces	225

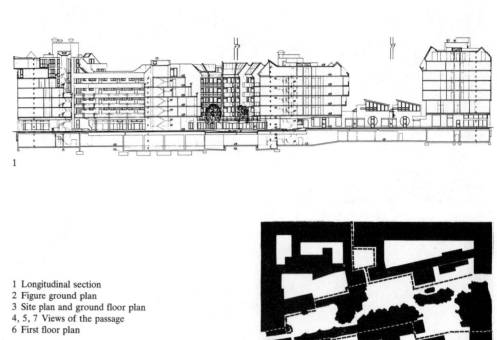

1 Longitudinal section
2 Figure ground plan
3 Site plan and ground floor plan
4, 5, 7 Views of the passage
6 First floor plan

ADALBERTSTRASSE

AMALIENPASSAGE
MÜNCHEN

1. OBERGESCHOSS
M   1 : 100

6

7

4

5

A. J. Diamond and Barton Myers: York Square, Toronto, CDN, 1969

Project Data

Site area	.2 ha	
Floor area	m²	

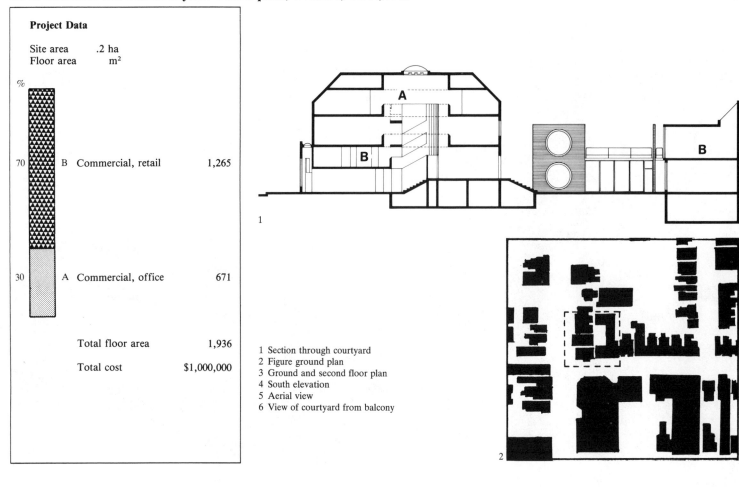

%				
70	B	Commercial, retail	1,265
30	A	Commercial, office	671
		Total floor area	1,936
		Total cost	$1,000,000

1 Section through courtyard
2 Figure ground plan
3 Ground and second floor plan
4 South elevation
5 Aerial view
6 View of courtyard from balcony

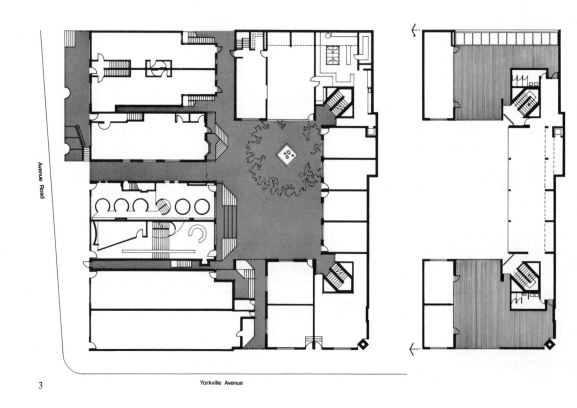

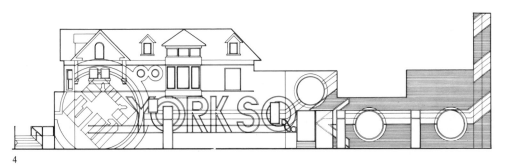

4

5

6

M. S. van Treeck, Ilot Riquet, Paris, F, 1969

Project Data

Site area   ca. 63.000 m²
Floor area   m²

%			m²
72	C	Residential	139,575
6.5	A	Commercial, office	13,400
17	O	Commons, public space	32,359
1,5	W	Community facilities	3,041
0,5	R	Educational	1,294
2	I	Merchandise mart	3,750
0,5	B	Commercial, retail	1,750

Total floor area		195,169
Residential units		1,896
Indoor parking spaces		2,060
Total cost	ca.FF	200,000,000

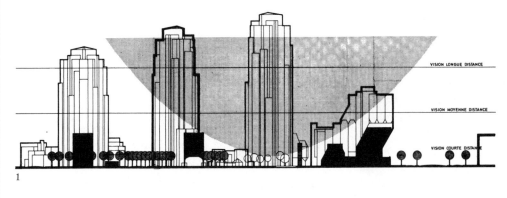

1

2

1 Vertical section
2 Site plan
3 Pedestrian zone, rue de Flandre
4 Master plan
5 Apartment tower
6 Main entrance, rue de Flandre

3

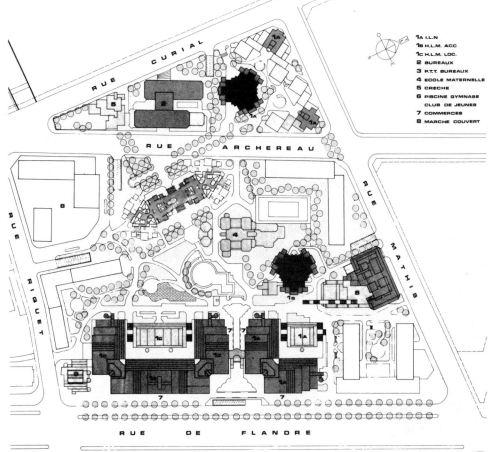

4

5

6

Peter Celsing: Culture House and Parliament Buildings, Stockholm, S, 1970

Project Data

Site area   .3 ha
Floor area   m²

E	Exhibition
A	Commercial, office
F	Recreational
G	Restaurant, cafeteria
D	Parking

Total floor area	118,000
Parliament	90,000
Cultural	28,000
Total cost	£18,000,000

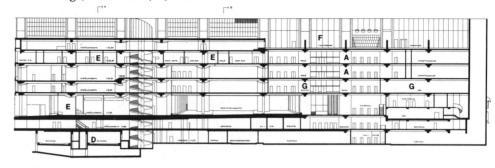

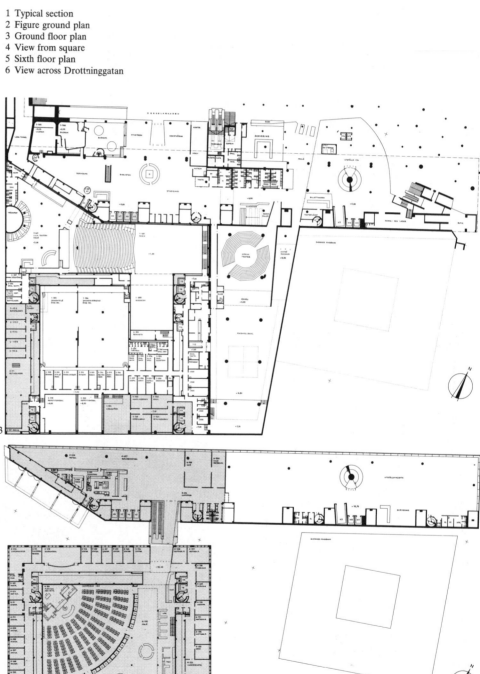

1 Typical section
2 Figure ground plan
3 Ground floor plan
4 View from square
5 Sixth floor plan
6 View across Drottninggatan

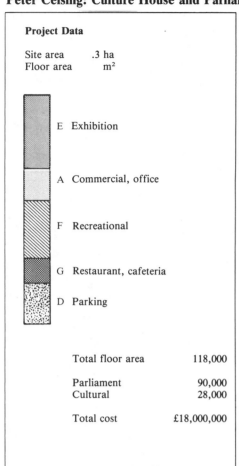

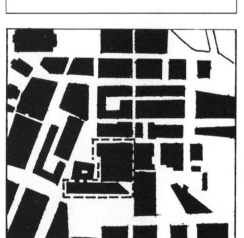

6

Gruen Associates, Cesar Pelli Partner in Charge: Commons + Courthouse Centre, Columbus, IN, USA, 1970

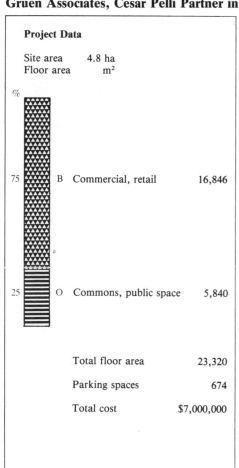

Project Data

Site area   4.8 ha
Floor area   m²

%			
75	B	Commercial, retail	16,846
25	O	Commons, public space	5,840
		Total floor area	23,320
		Parking spaces	674
		Total cost	$7,000,000

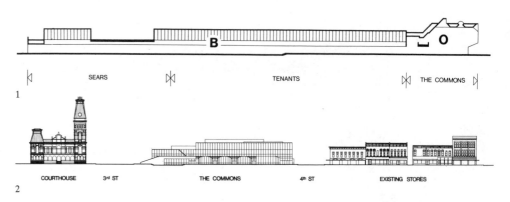

1 Longitudinal section
2 Washington Street elevation
3 Figure ground plan
4 Street level plan
5 Axonometric
6 View from Washington Street
7 View of Commons interior
8 Downtown development
9 Auto + pedestrian scales
10 Circulation
11 Pedestrian movement
12 Sidewalk space

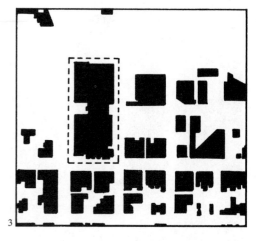

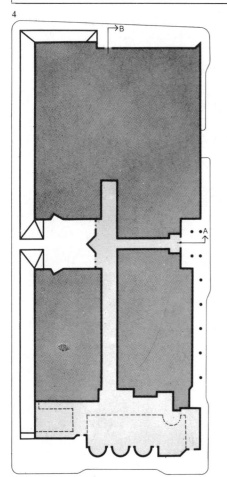

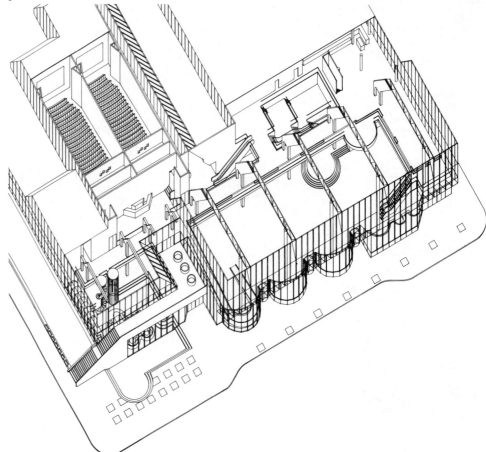

6

7

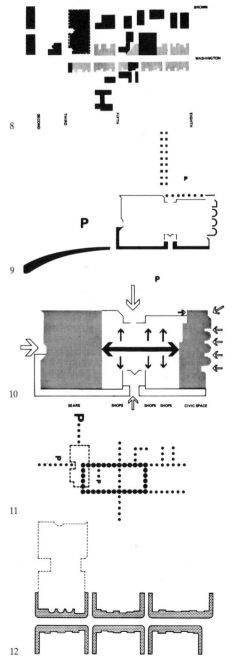

8

9

10

11

12

Hellmuth, Obata + Kassabaum, Inc.: The Galleria, Houston, TX, USA, 1971

Project Data

Site area   13.3 ha
Floor area   m²

%			
22	A	Commercial, office	32,236
50	B	Commercial, retail	73,205
21	J	Hotel	31,446
7	D	Club	9,626
		Total floor area	146,513
		Parking spaces	7,040

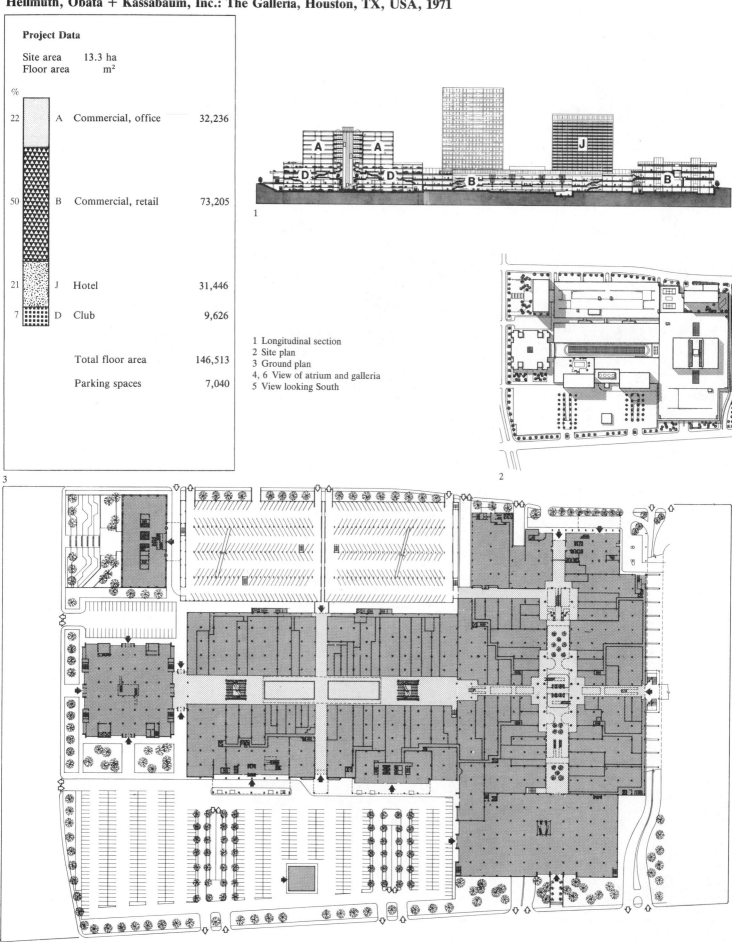

1 Longitudinal section
2 Site plan
3 Ground plan
4, 6 View of atrium and galleria
5 View looking South

4

5

6

Johnson, Burgee, Edward F. Baker Associates: I.D.S. Centre, Minneapolis, MN, USA, 1972

Project Data

Site area   10.1 ha
Floor area   m²

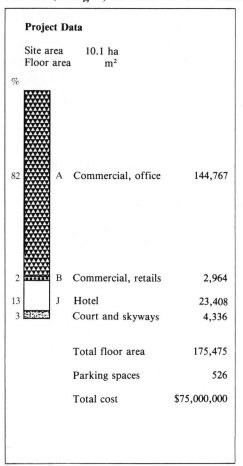

%			
82	A	Commercial, office	144,767
2	B	Commercial, retails	2,964
13	J	Hotel	23,408
3		Court and skyways	4,336
		Total floor area	175,475
		Parking spaces	526
		Total cost	$75,000,000

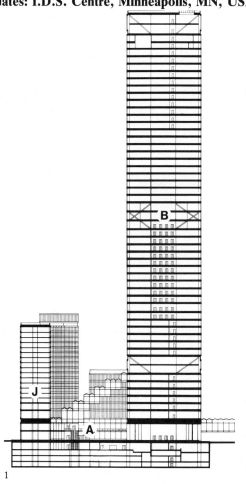

1

2

1 Typical section
2 Exterior view
3 Ground floor plan
4 Second floor plan
5 Tenth floor plan
6 View of interior atrium

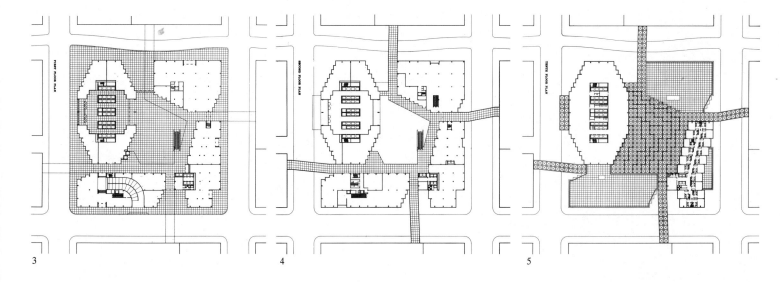

3

4

5

6

James Stirling: Derby Civic Centre Competition, Derby, GB, 1972

Project Data

Site area   2 ha
Floor area   m²

A   Commercial, office

U   Civic, convention center

B   Commercial, retail

Parking spaces   624

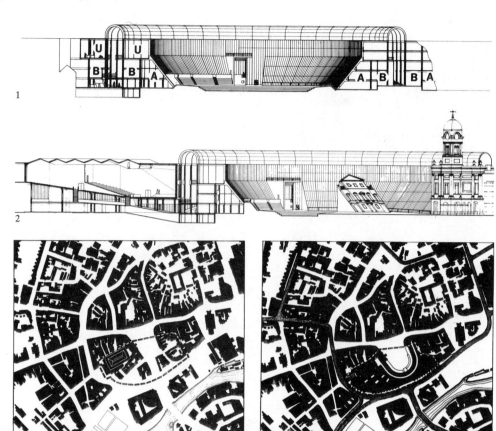

1

2

3

4

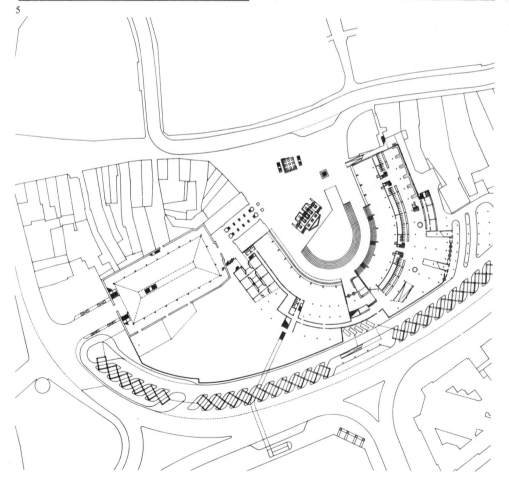

5

1 Typical section
2 Section facing square
3 Figure ground, existing city centre
4 Figure ground, new ring road and pedestrian centre
5 Ground floor plan
6 Elevation from square
7 Perspective of gallery
8 Diagram of plaza
9 Third floor plan
10 Fourth floor plan
11 Fifth + sixth floor plan

38

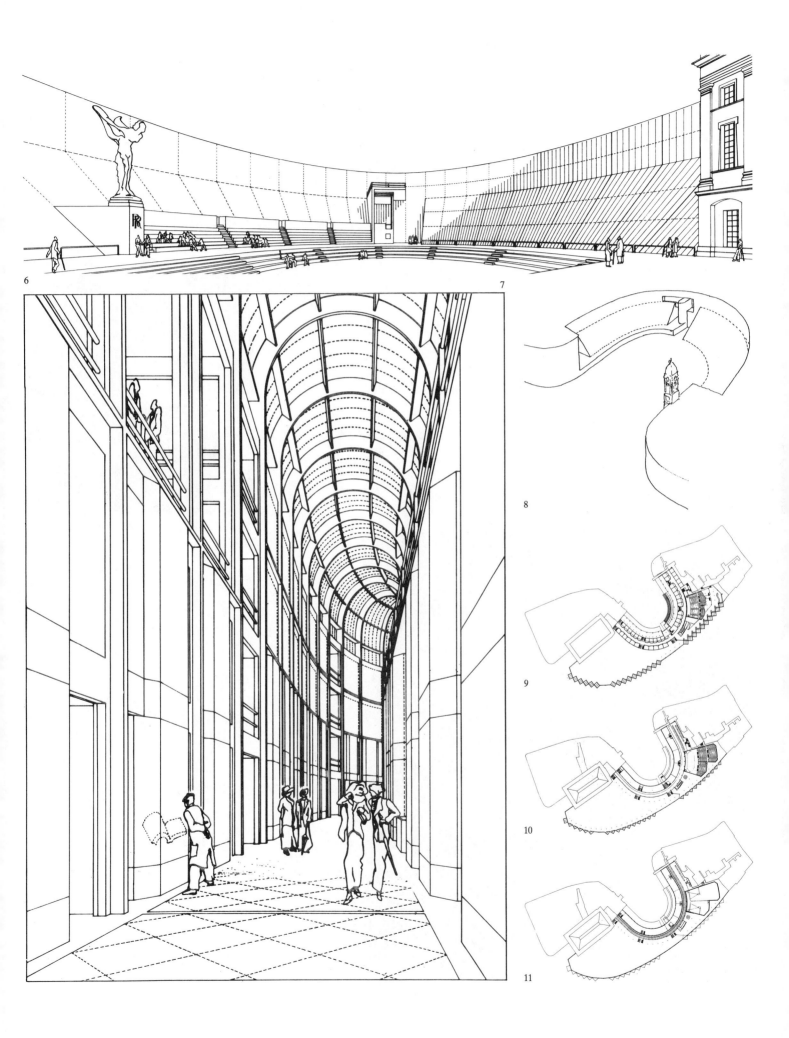

6

7

8

9

10

11

Chapman Taylor Partners: Eldon Square Shopping and Recreation Centre, New Castle, GB, 1972

Project Data

Site area   4.32 ha
Floor area   m²

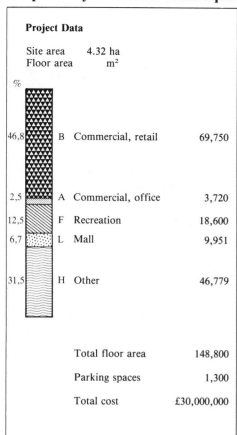

%			
46,8	B	Commercial, retail	69,750
2,5	A	Commercial, office	3,720
12,5	F	Recreation	18,600
6,7	L	Mall	9,951
31,5	H	Other	46,779

Total floor area	148,800
Parking spaces	1,300
Total cost	£30,000,000

1

1 North-South section
2 Figure ground plan
3 Site plan
4 Mall level plan
5 West-East section
6 Northern concourse with elevated coffee shop
7 Exterior view from Eldon Square
8 View of typical mall

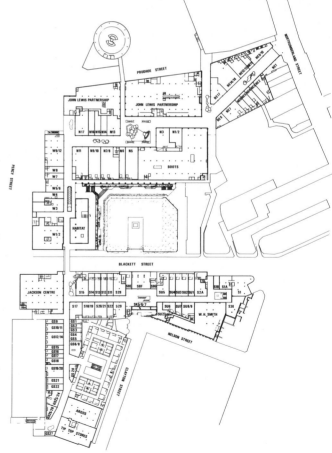

2

3

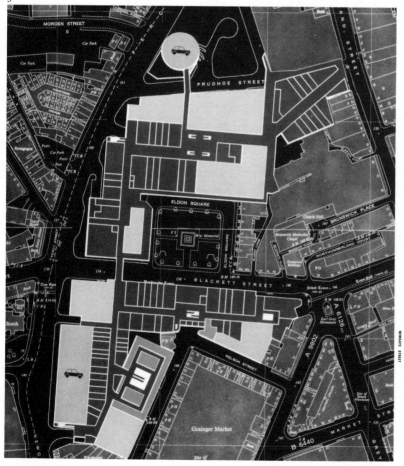

4

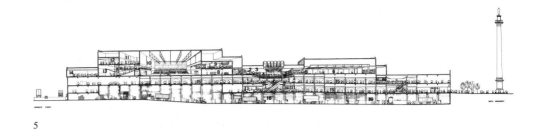

5

6

7

8

A. J. Diamond & Barton Myers in Association with R. L. Wilkin: Housing Union Building, Edmonton, CDN, 1973

Project Data

Site area	2.9 ha	
Floor area	m²	

%				
5	B	Commercial, retail		1,860
85	C	Residential		30,033
10	H	Other		3,447
		Total floor area		35,340

Residential units

94	=	4 pers.
188	=	2 pers.
236	=	1 pers.
Total 518		

Total cost	$5,600,000

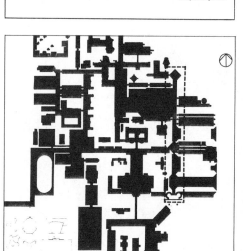

1 Section
2 Figure ground plan
3 Aerial view of site
4 Aerial view of campus
5 Unit plans and corresponding axonometrics
6 Galleria level plan
7 Elevation
8 Interior mall

1

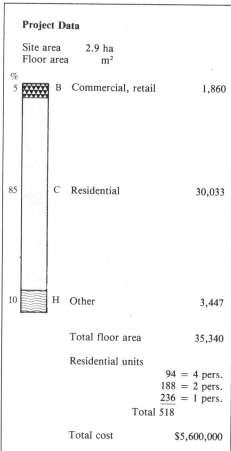

2

3

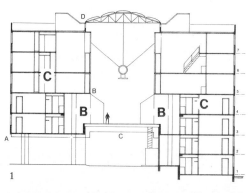

4

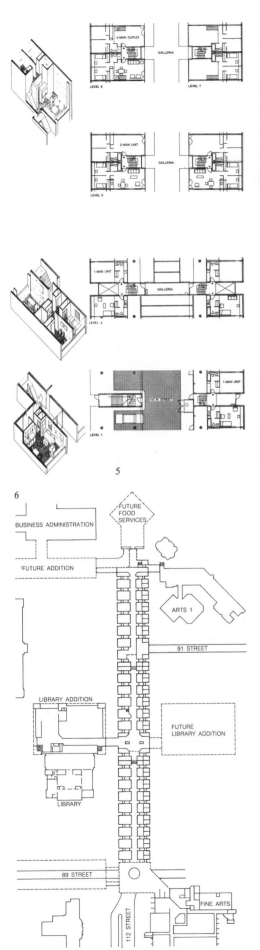

John Portman & Associates: Peachtree Centre, Atlanta, GA, USA, 1973

Project Data

Site area	4.05 ha	
developed	1.21 ha	
Floor area	m²	
Commercial, retail		21,669
Commercial, office		
— 230 Peachtree Center Tower		30,690
— Gas light tower		25,469
— South tower		24,208
— Cain tower		30,968
— Harris tower		30,790
Merchandise mart		186,000
Entertainment		
Seat theatre		500
Hotel units		
— Hyatt Regency Hotel		1,000
— Plaza Hotel		1,100
Parking spaces		1,500
Total cost		ca. $250,000,000

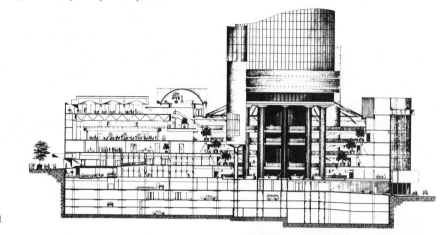

1

1 Section through lower floors of Plaza Hotel
2 Figure ground plan
3 Site plan and ground floor plan of Plaza Hotel
4 View of Peachtree Plaza Hotel
5 Aerial view towards Ivy Street
6 View of bridge to mart
7 Street level view of office tower

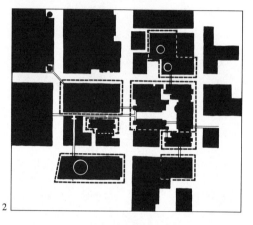

2

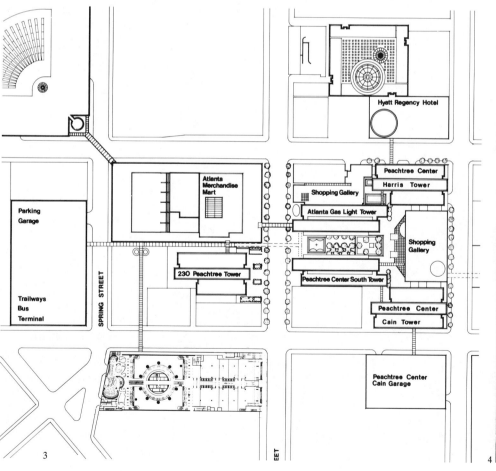

3

4

5

6

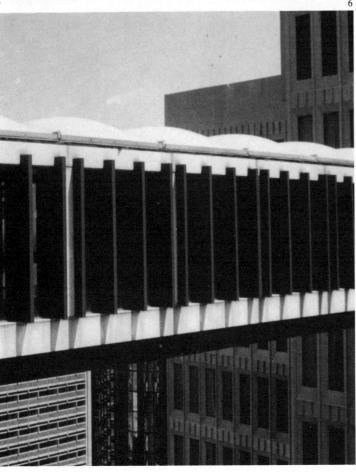

7

8 View of interior mall
9 View of Hyatt Regency Hotel
10 Plan of main hall
11 Plan of typical hotel floor
   Plan of restaurant
   Plan of access level to roof restaurant
12 Plan of Spring Street level
13 Interior view of Hyatt Regency Hotel
14 Interior view of Plaza Hotel

8

9

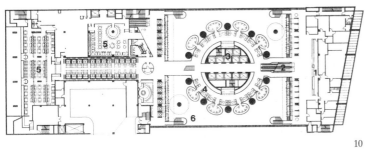

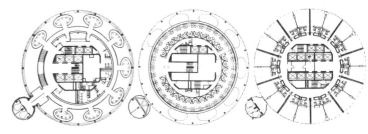

10

11

14

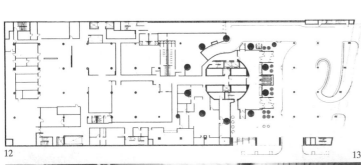

12

13

Thompson, Ventulett, Stainback & Associates: Omni International, Atlanta, GA, USA, 1973

Project Data		
Site area	2.3 ha	
Floor area	m²	

%				
38	A	Commercial, office	59,868
19	B	Commercial, retail	28,989
27	J	Hotel	41,875
8	F	Recreational	12,842
8	D	Parking	12,908
		Total floor area	156,482
		Total cost	$70,000,000

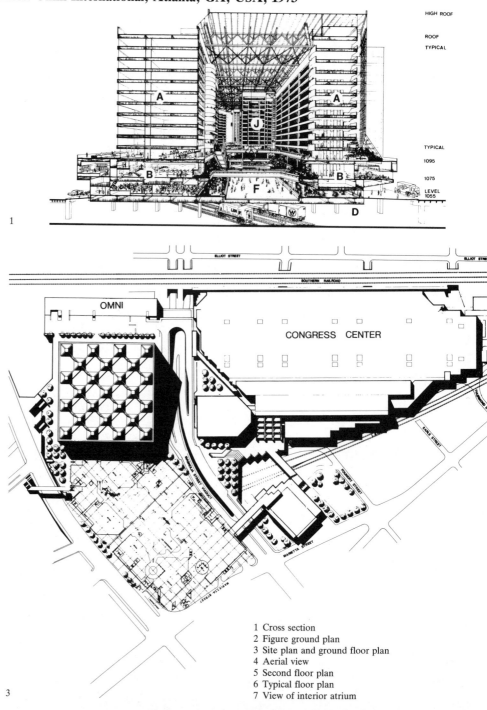

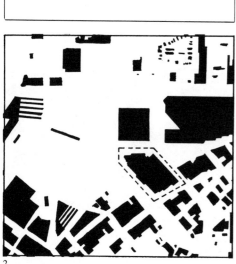

1 Cross section
2 Figure ground plan
3 Site plan and ground floor plan
4 Aerial view
5 Second floor plan
6 Typical floor plan
7 View of interior atrium

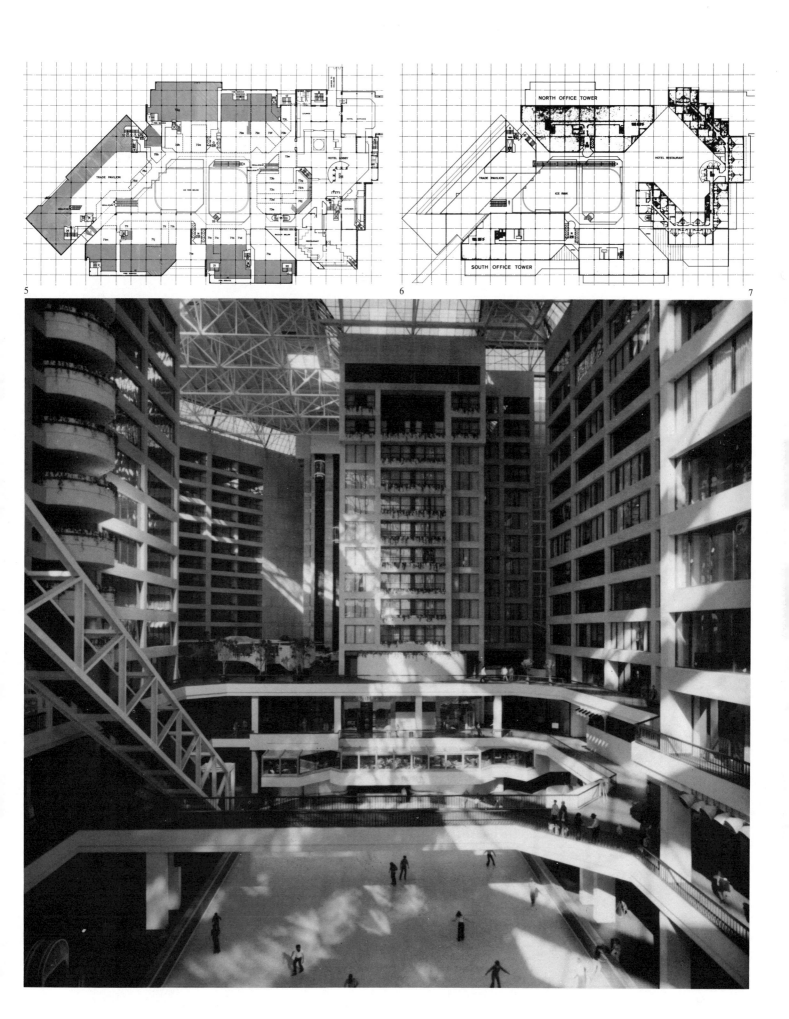

5   6   7

Elbasani, Logan, Severin: Kalamazoo Centre, Kalamazoo, MI, USA, 1974

Project Data

Site area   .8 ha
Floor area   m²

%				m²
20	B	Commercial, retail		6,696
8	A	Commercial, office		2,790
55	J	Hotel		18,600
17	U	Civic, convention center		5,580

Total floor area	33,666
Hotel units	288
Indoor parking spaces	1,050
Separate building	
Total cost	ca. $25,000,000

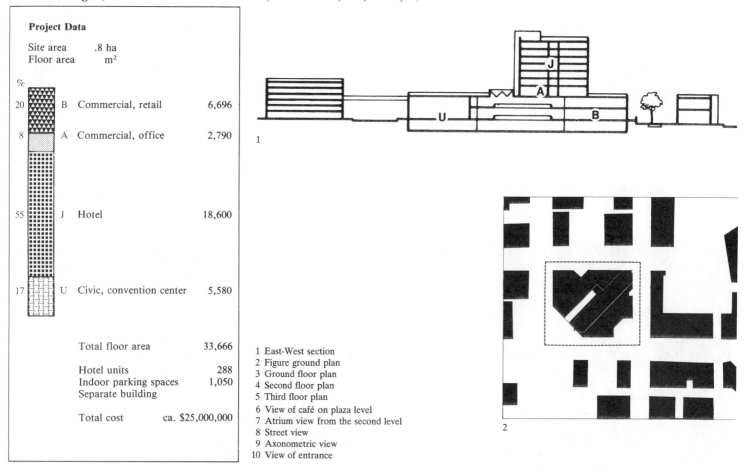

1 East-West section
2 Figure ground plan
3 Ground floor plan
4 Second floor plan
5 Third floor plan
6 View of café on plaza level
7 Atrium view from the second level
8 Street view
9 Axonometric view
10 View of entrance

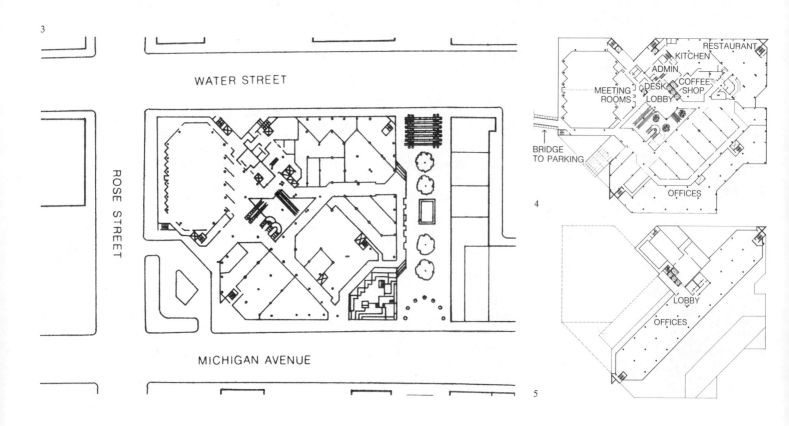

WATER STREET

ROSE STREET

MICHIGAN AVENUE

BRIDGE TO PARKING

RESTAURANT
KITCHEN
ADMIN
MEETING ROOMS
DESK
LOBBY
COFFEE SHOP
OFFICES

LOBBY
OFFICES

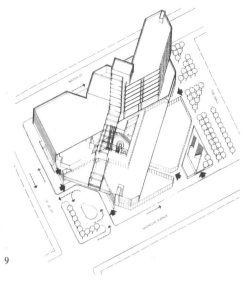

9

6

7

8

10

Hugh Stubbins & Associates: Citicorp Centre, New York, NY, USA, 1974

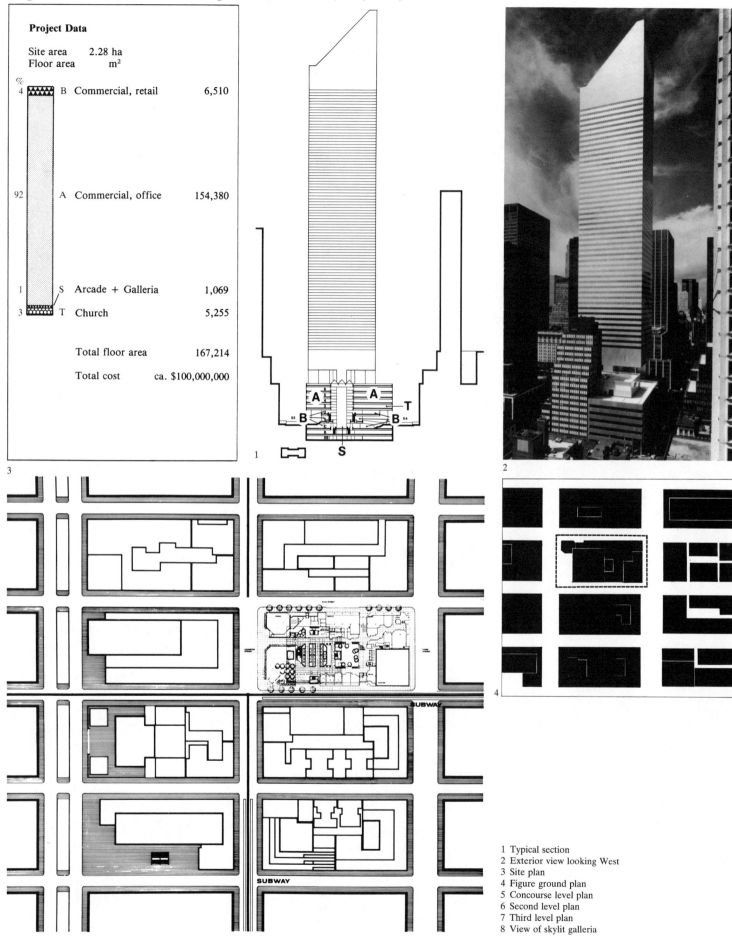

Project Data

Site area	2.28 ha				
Floor area	m²				

%				
4	B	Commercial, retail	6,510	
92	A	Commercial, office	154,380	
1	S	Arcade + Galleria	1,069	
3	T	Church	5,255	
		Total floor area	167,214	
		Total cost	ca. $100,000,000	

1 Typical section
2 Exterior view looking West
3 Site plan
4 Figure ground plan
5 Concourse level plan
6 Second level plan
7 Third level plan
8 View of skylit galleria

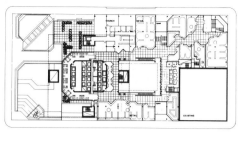
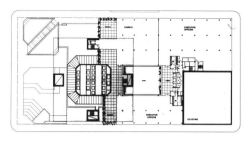

5

6

7

8

Gottfried Böhm, Hans Linder: Bürgerhaus "Bergischer Löwe", Bergisch Gladbach, D, 1975

Project Data

Site area
Floor area   m²

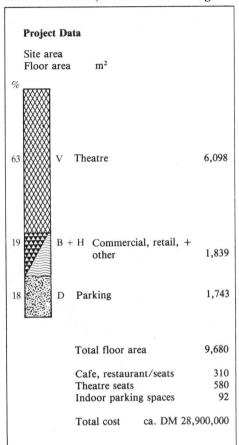

%			
63	V	Theatre	6,098
19	B + H	Commercial, retail, + other	1,839
18	D	Parking	1,743
		Total floor area	9,680
		Cafe, restaurant/seats	310
		Theatre seats	580
		Indoor parking spaces	92
		Total cost	ca. DM 28,900,000

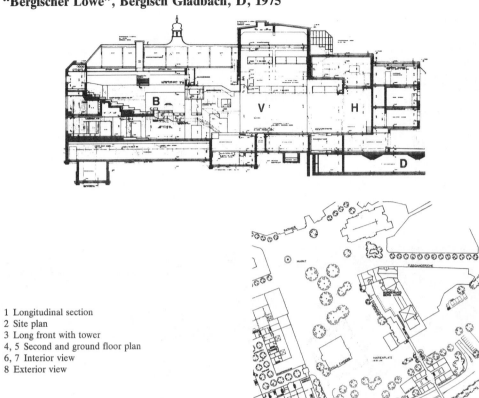

1 Longitudinal section
2 Site plan
3 Long front with tower
4, 5 Second and ground floor plan
6, 7 Interior view
8 Exterior view

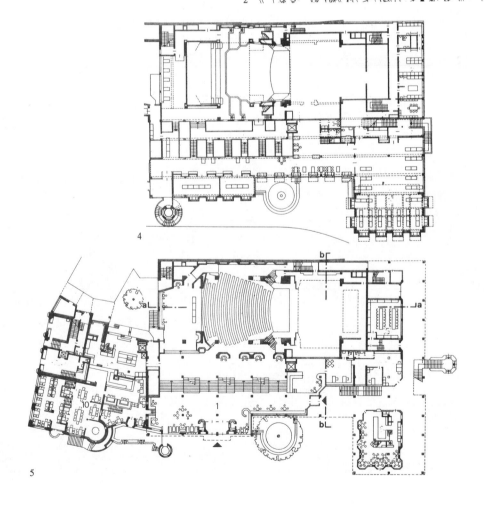

6

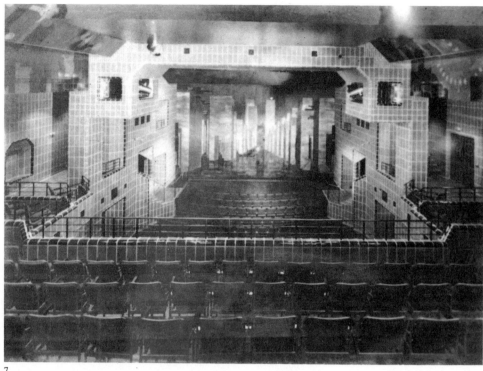

7

8

Cossutta & Associates: Credit Lyonnais Tower, Lyon, F, 1975

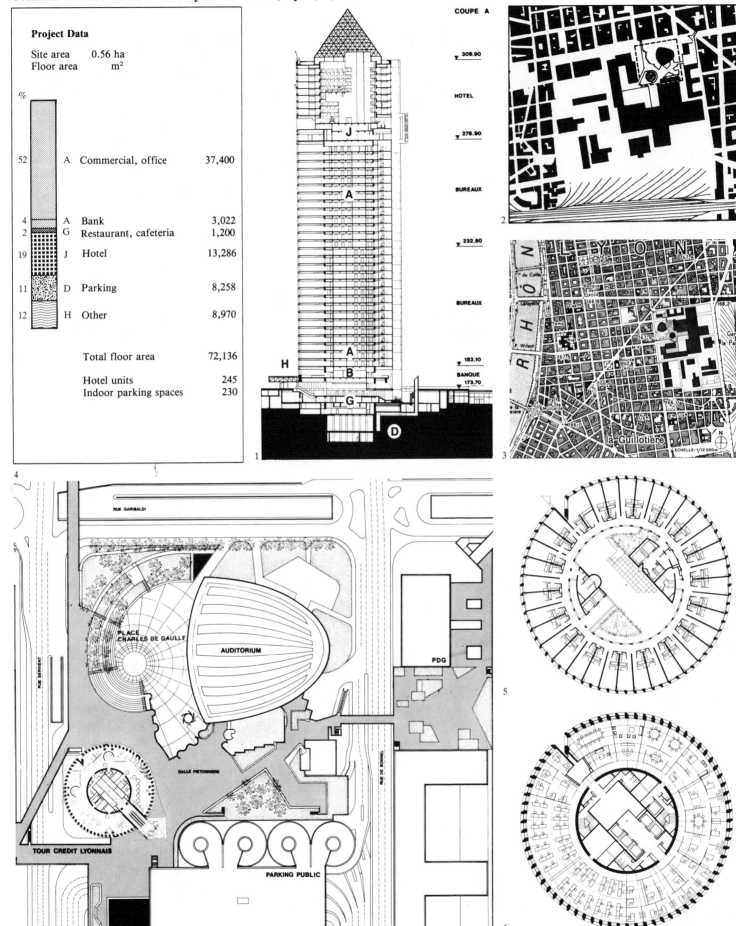

Project Data

Site area	0.56 ha			
Floor area	m²			

%				m²
52	A	Commercial, office		37,400
4	A	Bank		3,022
2	G	Restaurant, cafeteria		1,200
19	J	Hotel		13,286
11	D	Parking		8,258
12	H	Other		8,970
		Total floor area		72,136
		Hotel units		245
		Indoor parking spaces		230

COUPE A

309.90
HOTEL
276.90
BUREAUX
232.60
BUREAUX
183.10
BANQUE
173.70

RUE GARIBALDI

PLACE CHARLES DE GAULLE

AUDITORIUM

PDG

SALLE PIETONNIERE

RUE SERVIENT

RUE DE BONNEL

TOUR CREDIT LYONNAIS

PARKING PUBLIC

1 2 3 4 5 6

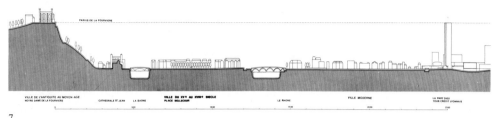

7

8

9

57

Eller – Moser – Walter + Partner: Kirchenforum, Bochum, D, 1975

Project Data

Site area   8 ha
Floor area   m²

%			
10	T	Church	1,060
22	W	Community facilities	2,310
14	X	Forum	1,440
37	C	Residential	3,850
10	B	Commercial, retail	1,040
3	S	Arcade + galleria	290
4	P	Technical spaces	370
		Total floor area	10,360
		Parking spaces	122

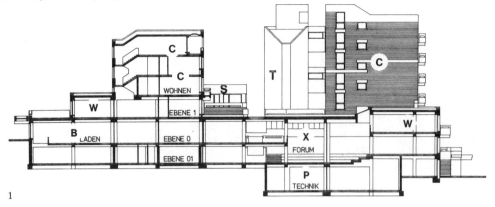

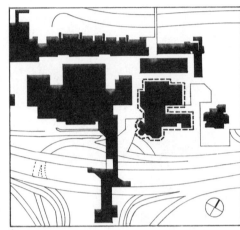

1

2

3

1 Section A-A
2 Exterior view
3 Figure ground plan
4 Axonometric, site plan
5 Level 0 plan
6 Level 1 plan
7 Level 2 plan
8 Exterior view

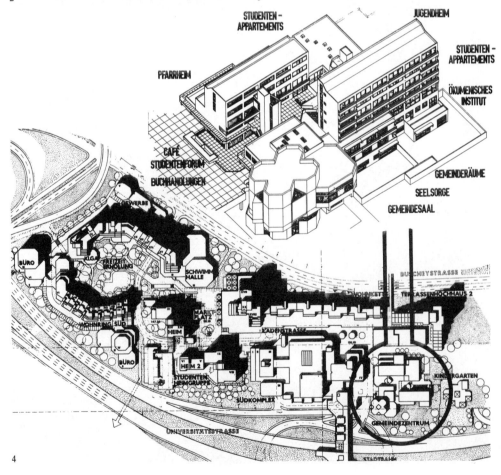

4

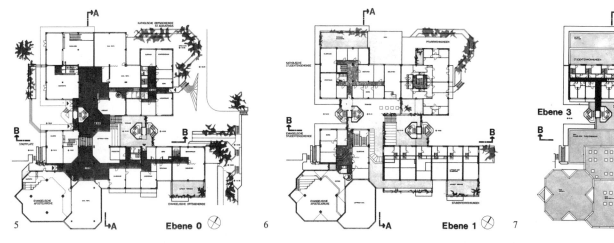

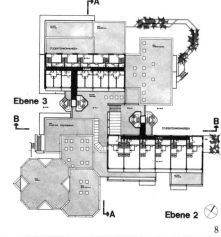

5   Ebene 0 ⊗   6   Ebene 1 ⊗   7   Ebene 2 ⊗

8

Elsom, Pack + Roberts: Victoria Square, London, GB, 1975

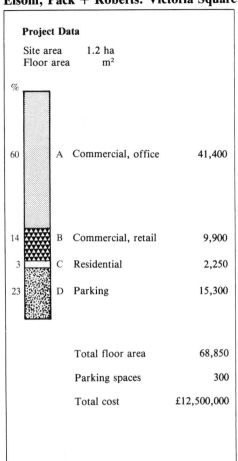

Project Data

Site area	1.2 ha	
Floor area	m²	

%			
60	A	Commercial, office	41,400
14	B	Commercial, retail	9,900
3	C	Residential	2,250
23	D	Parking	15,300
		Total floor area	68,850
		Parking spaces	300
		Total cost	£12,500,000

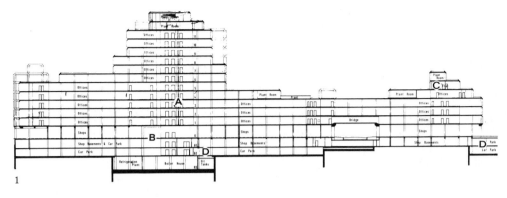

1 Longitudinal section
2 Figure ground plan
3, 4, 5 Ground floor, 2nd and 3rd floor plan
6 View of model
7 Looking north
8 View from Ashley Place

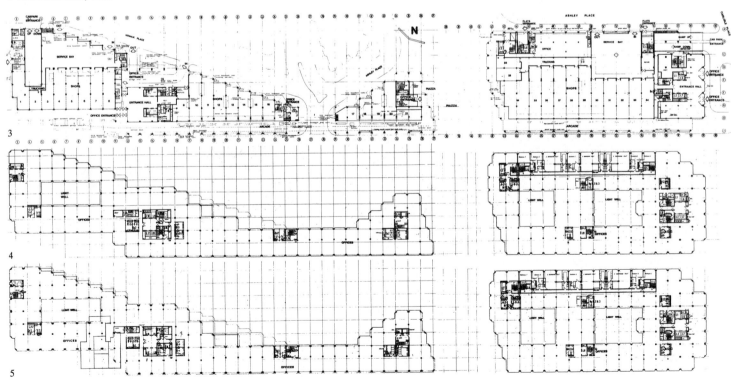

6

7

8

Graaf – Schweger + Partner: Kaufmannshaus, Hamburg, D, 1975/76

Project Data

Site area   4.539m²
Floor area   m²

%			
75	A	Commercial, office	18,000
13,3	B	Commercial, retail	3,200
11,7	P	Technical, spaces	2,800
		Total floor area	24,000
		Total cost ca. DM	40,000,000

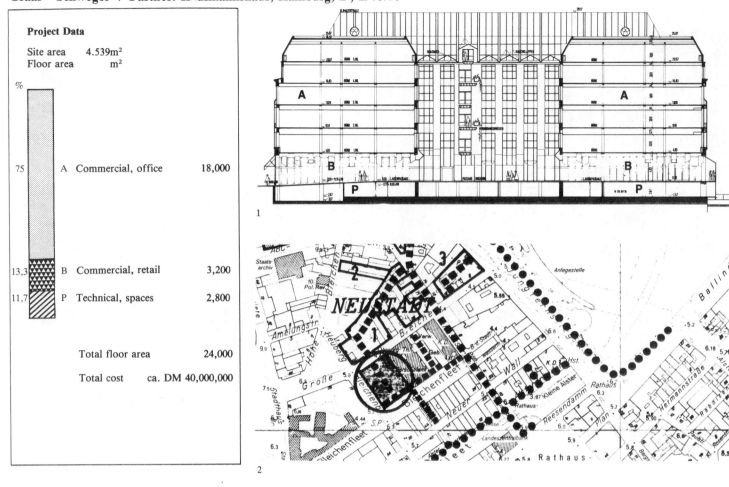

1

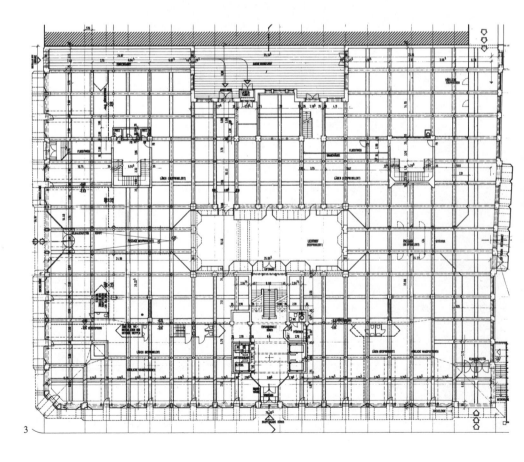

2

1 Section
2 Figure ground plan
3 Ground floor plan
4 Interior view of ground and mezzanine level
5 View from Große Bleichen and Bleichenbrücke
6 Perspective view before renovation
7 Bleichenfleet elevation

3

4

5

6

7

Ole Meyer, Bella Centre, Copenhagen, DK, 1975

Project Data

Site area   28 ha
Floor area   m²

%				m²
34	I	Merchandise mart		26,000
21	A + G	Commercial, office, restaurant		15,800
38	E	Exhibition		28,800
7	U	Civic, convention center		5,510
		Total floor area		76,110
		Total cost	DKR	220,000,000

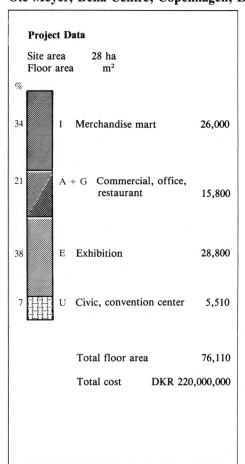

1

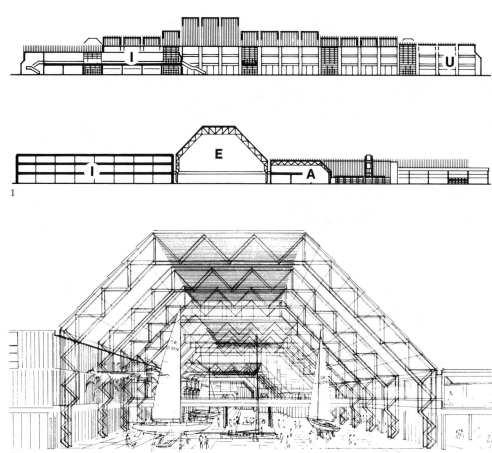

2

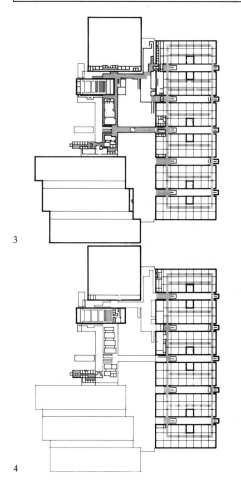

3

4

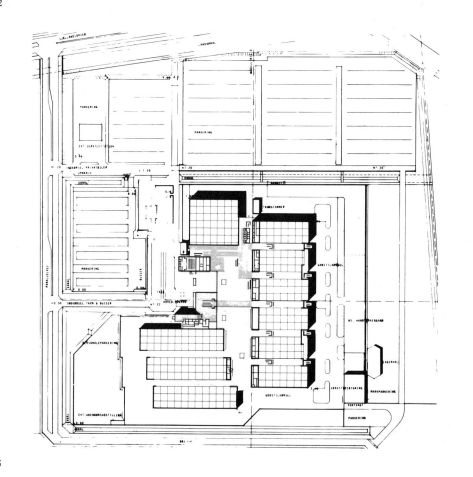

5

6

7

1 Longitudinal sections
2 Cross section
3 Second floor plan
4 Third floor plan
5 Site plan with ground floor plan
6 View of exhibition area
7 + 8 Exterior views

8

Richard Meier & Associates: Alamo Plaza Colorado Springs, CO, USA, 1978

Project Data

Site area 1.6 ha
Floor area m²

%		
20	A	Commercial, office
15	B	Commercial, retail
35	U	Civic, convention center
10	J	Hotel
10	C	Residential
5	F	Recreational

Parking spaces 1,000

Total cost $25,000,000

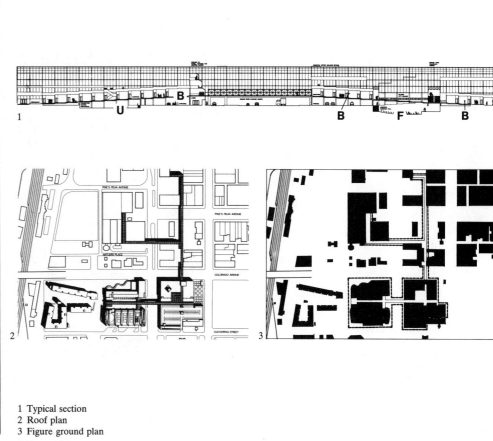

1

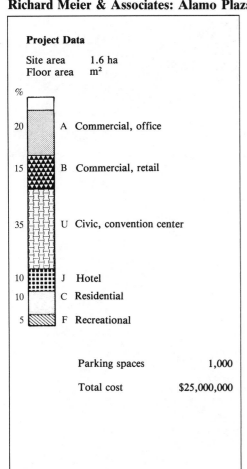

4

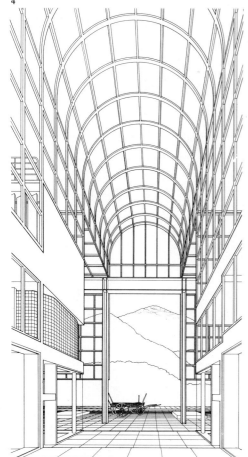

2

3

1 Typical section
2 Roof plan
3 Figure ground plan
4 Perspective
5 Ground floor plan

5

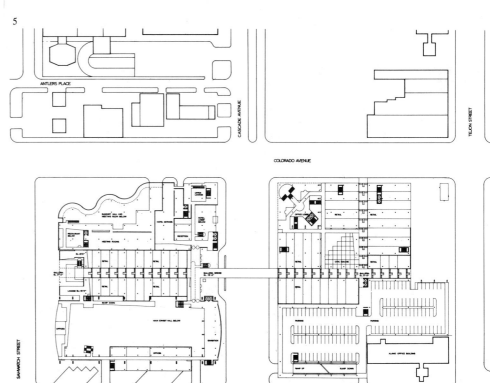

Loebl, Schlossman, Dart & Hackl: Water Tower Place, Chicago, IL, USA

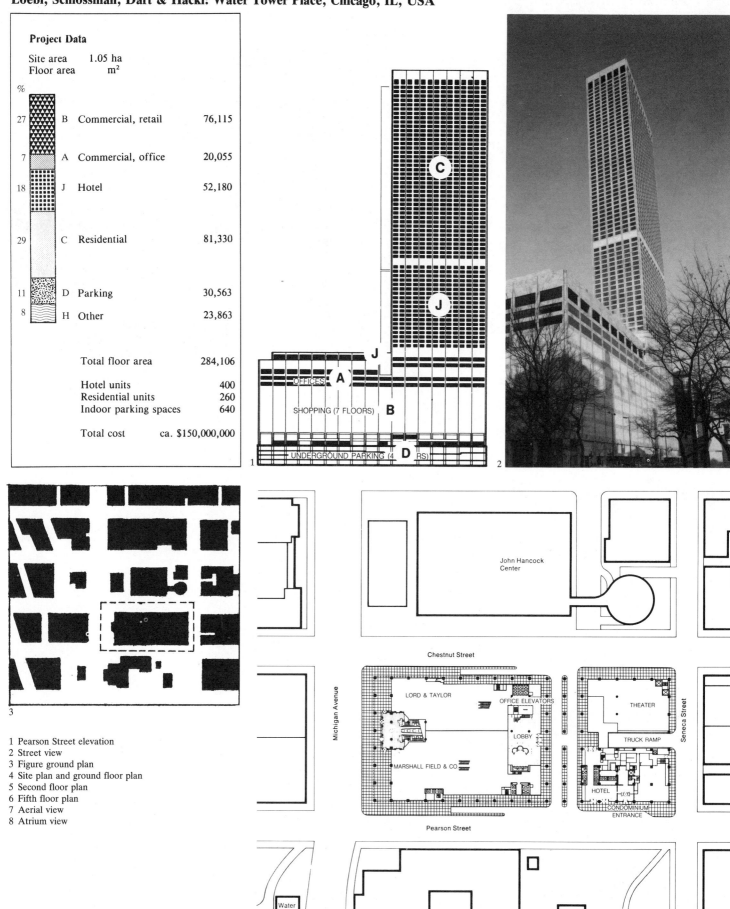

Project Data

%				
	Site area	1.05 ha		
	Floor area	m²		
27	B	Commercial, retail	76,115	
7	A	Commercial, office	20,055	
18	J	Hotel	52,180	
29	C	Residential	81,330	
11	D	Parking	30,563	
8	H	Other	23,863	

Total floor area	284,106	
Hotel units	400	
Residential units	260	
Indoor parking spaces	640	
Total cost	ca. $150,000,000	

1 Pearson Street elevation
2 Street view
3 Figure ground plan
4 Site plan and ground floor plan
5 Second floor plan
6 Fifth floor plan
7 Aerial view
8 Atrium view

68

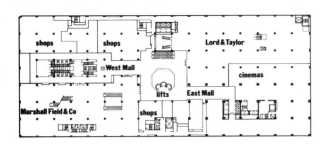

5

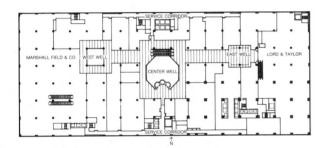

6

7

8

David Specter: Galleria, New York, NY, USA, 1975

Project Data

%			m²
17	A	Commercial, office	7,432
5	B	Commercial, retail	2,323
78	C	Residential	32,050

Site area .3 ha
Floor area m²

Total floor area 41,805

Indoor parking spaces 94

Total cost ca. $50,000,000

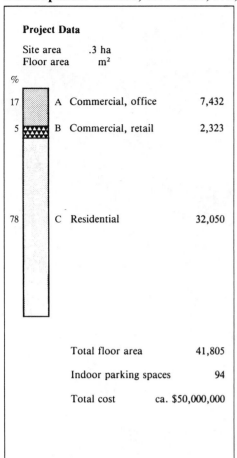

1

2

1 Longitudinal section
2 Street view
3 Typical floor plan
4 Site plan and ground floor plan
5 Aerial view
6 View of atrium

3

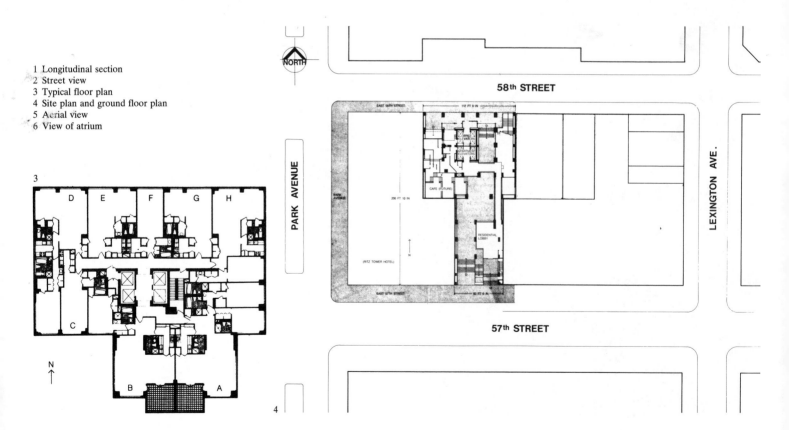

4

5

6

The Architects Collaborative; Concept Development Herman H. Field: Josiah Quincy School, Boston, MA, USA, 1976

Project Data

Site area   1.4 ha
Floor area   m²

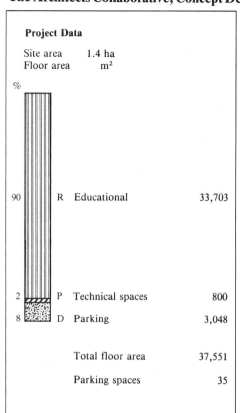

90	R Educational	33,703
2	P Technical spaces	800
8	D Parking	3,048
	Total floor area	37,551
	Parking spaces	35

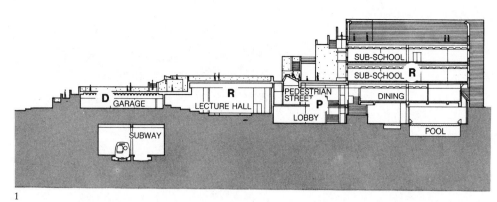

1

1 Longitudinal section
2 View of interior
3 Site plan and ground floor plan
4 Basement floor plan
5 Second floor plan
6 Third floor plan
7 View of roof

2

3

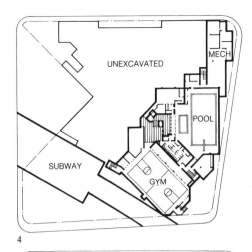

4

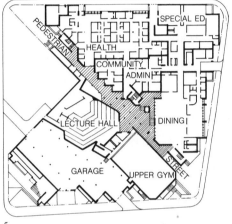

5

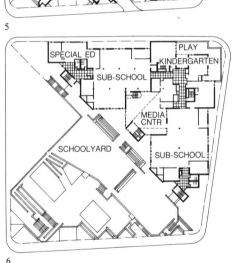

6

7

John Sharratt & Associates: Mercantile Wharf Building, Boston, MA, USA, 1976

Project Data

Site area   .4 ha
Floor area   m²

%			m²
81	C	Residential	12,690
8	A	Commercial, office	1,209
6	M	Atrium + lobby	885
5	N	Lounges	800
		Total floor area	17,704
		Total cost	$5,100,000

1 Typical section
2 Figure ground plan
3 Third floor plan
4 Site plan and ground floor plan
5 View of interior atrium
6 View across park
7 View of corridor

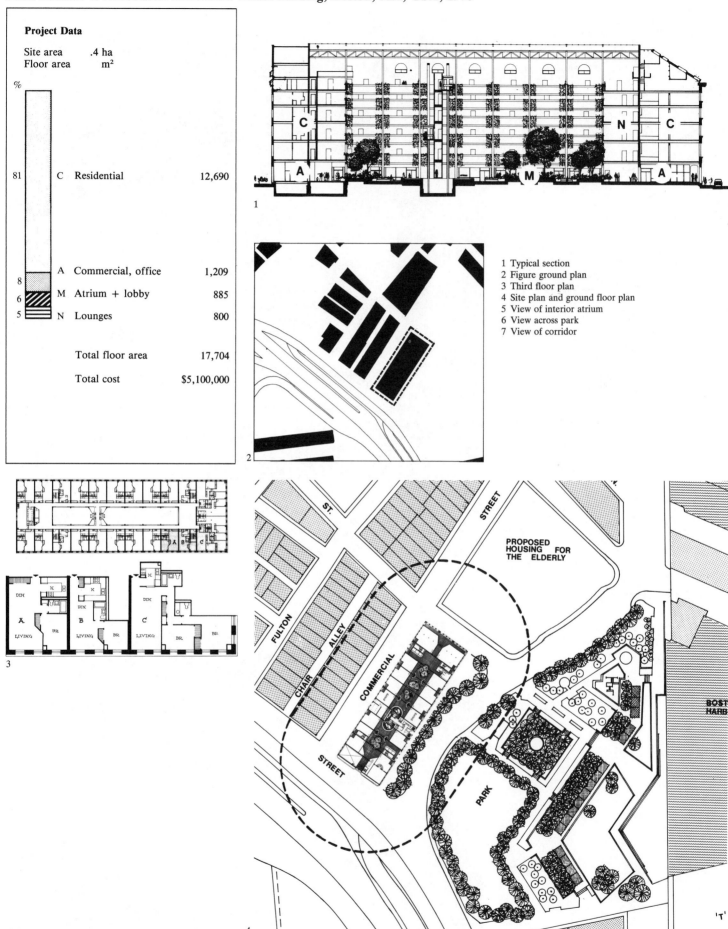

74

5

6

7

M. S. van Treeck: Centre Urbain Murat, Laval, F, 1976

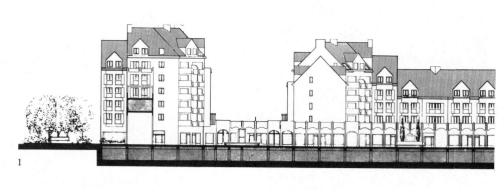

Project Data		
Site area	2.0 ha	
Floor area	m²	

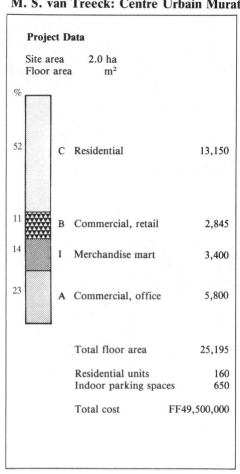

C	Residential	13,150
B	Commercial, retail	2,845
I	Merchandise mart	3,400
A	Commercial, office	5,800
	Total floor area	25,195
	Residential units	160
	Indoor parking spaces	650
	Total cost	FF49,500,000

1

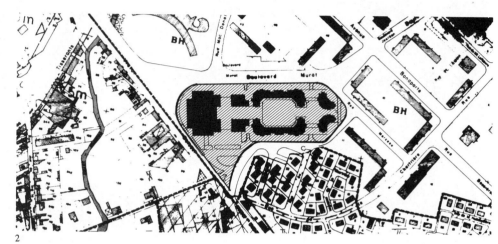

2

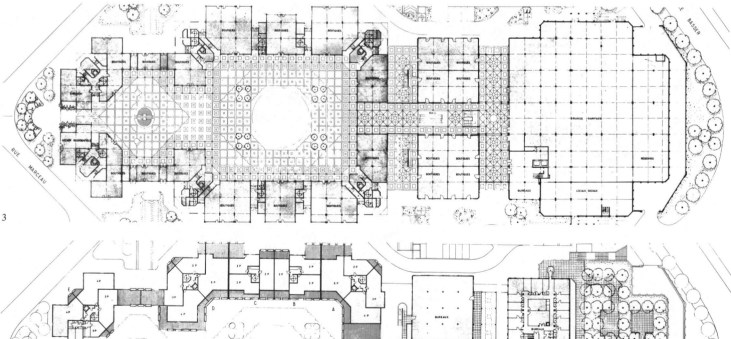

3

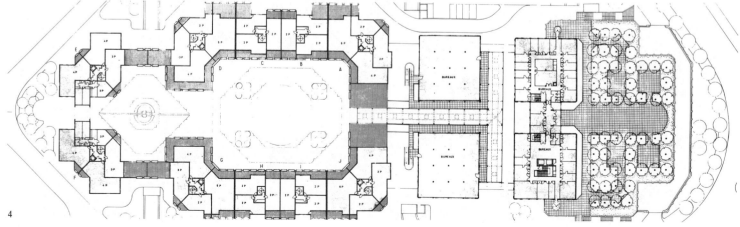

4

76

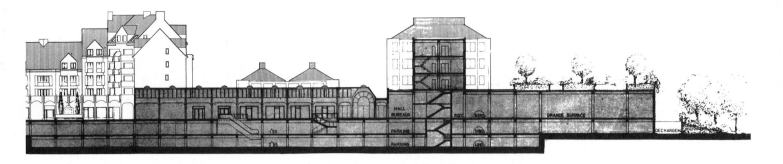

1 Section
2 Siteplan
3 Ground floor plan
4 First floor plan
5 Exterior view
6 Model

5

6

The Zeidler Partnership: Century Place, Bellville, CDN, 1976

Project Data

Site area   1.4 ha
Floor area   m²

%			
42	A	Commercial, office	5,000
36	B	Commercial, retail	4,249
22	D	Parking	2,700
		Total floor area	11,949
		Total cost	$2,600,000

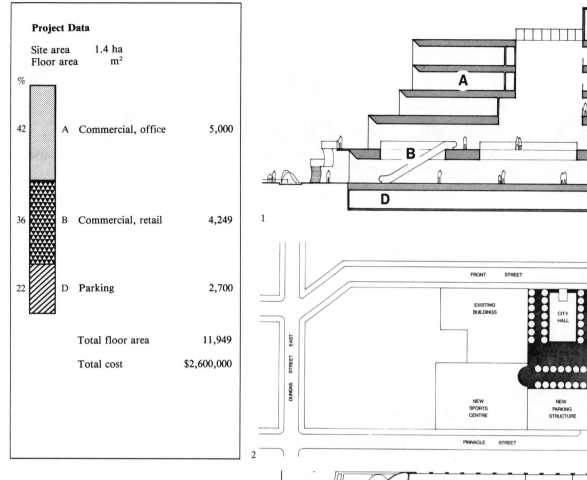

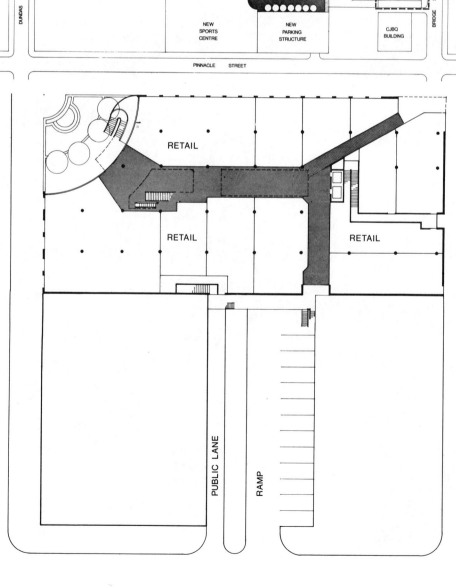

1 Typical section
2 Figure ground plan
3 Ground floor plan
4 View of interior atrium from balcony
5 View of exterior from Bridge Street
6 View across corner

4

5

6

Bregmann + Hamann & Zeidler Partnership (Design E. H. Zeidler): Toronto Eaton Centre, Toronto, CDN, 1978

Project Data

Site area 5.86 ha
Floor area m²

%				m²
54	A	Commercial, office		138,086
21	B	Commercial, retail		54,134
4	C/J	Residential, hotel		8,723
21	D	Parking		54,585
		Total floor area		255,528
		Parking spaces		1,490

1 Longitudinal section
2 Figure ground plan
3 Site plan and ground floor plan
4 Section looking North
5 Section looking South
6, 8 View of exterior on Yonge Street
7 Interior view
9 View of galleria
10 Dundas Court
11 View of galleria looking South

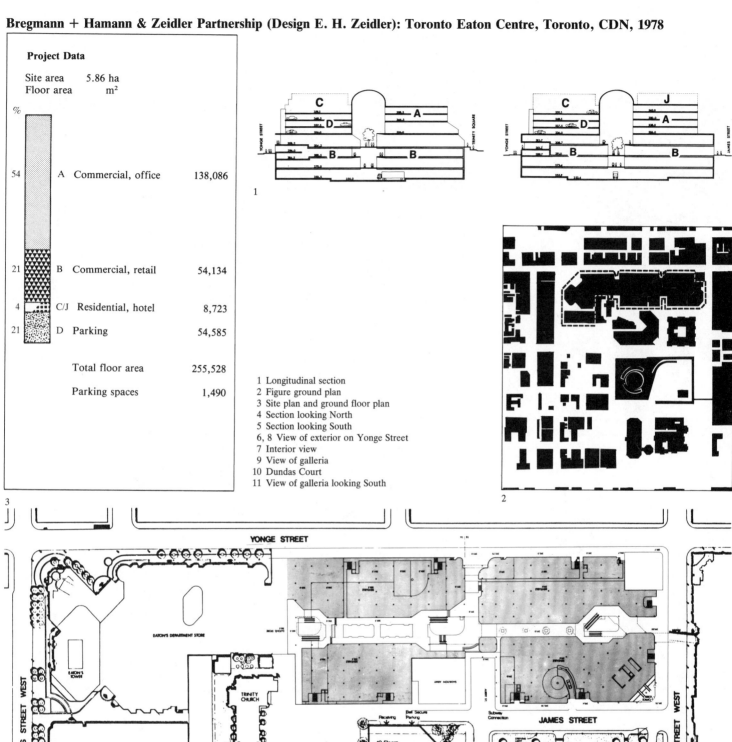

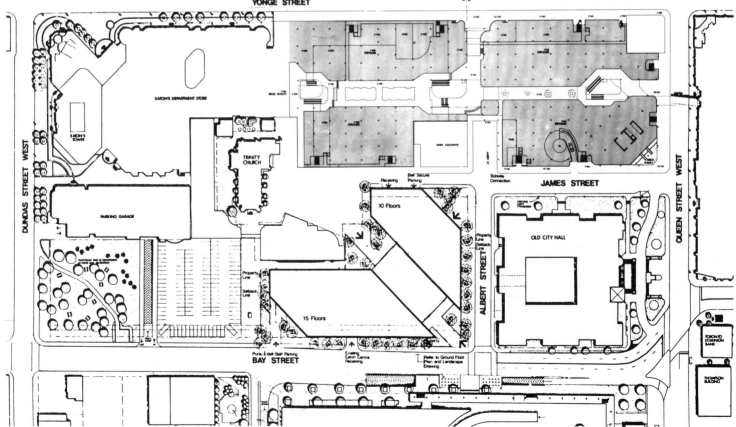

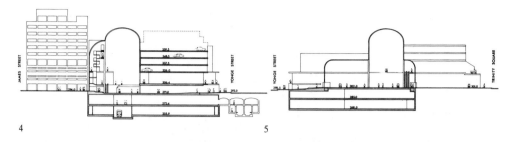

4

5

6

7

9

8

10

11

Kammerer + Belz und Partner: Calwer Straße, Stuttgart, D, 1978

Project Data

Site area   4.222m²
Floor area   m²

%				
23		A	Commercial, office	4,200
30		B	Commercial, retail	5,400
12		C	Residential	2,150
22		D	Parking	3,900
13		H	Other	2,400
			Total floor area	18,050
			Residential units	36
			Indoor parking spaces	108
			Total cost	DM 57,000,000

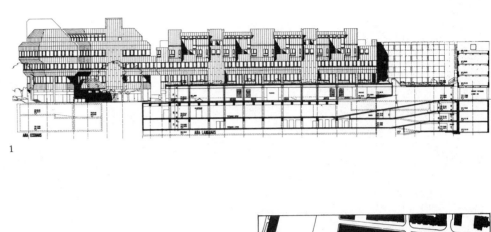

1

2

1 Longitudinal section
2 Figure ground plan
3 Ground floor plan
4 Latitudinal section
5, 6 Housing and offices above passage
7 Exterior view of passage and housing above
8 Third floor plan
9 Interior view of passage

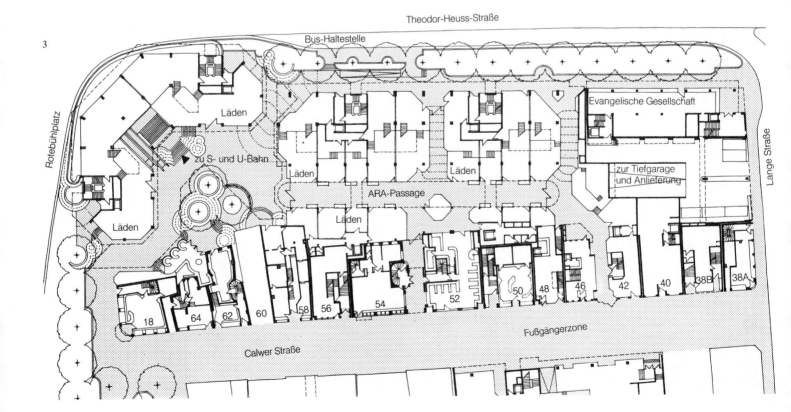

3

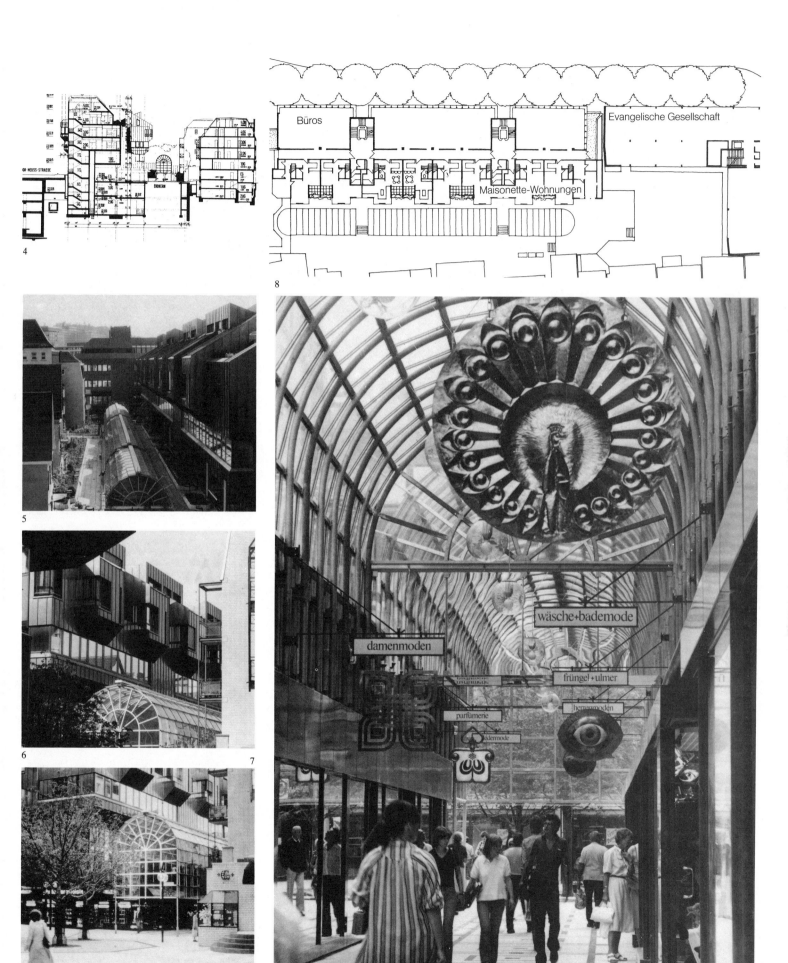

4

8

Büros

Evangelische Gesellschaft

Maisonette-Wohnungen

5

6

7

9

damenmoden

wäsche+bademode

frängel+ulmer

parfümerie

herrenmoden

bademode

Irving Grossman: Jarvis/Wilson Building, St. Lawrence, Phase A, Toronto, CDN, 1979

Project Data

Site area		.7 ha	
Floor area		m²	

%				
63	C	Residential	42,946
17	R	Educational	11,947
7	B	Commercial, retail	4,557
8	D	Parking	5,217
5	W	Community facilities	3,767

Total floor area	68,434
Residential units	207
Parking spaces	52
Total cost	$6,000,000

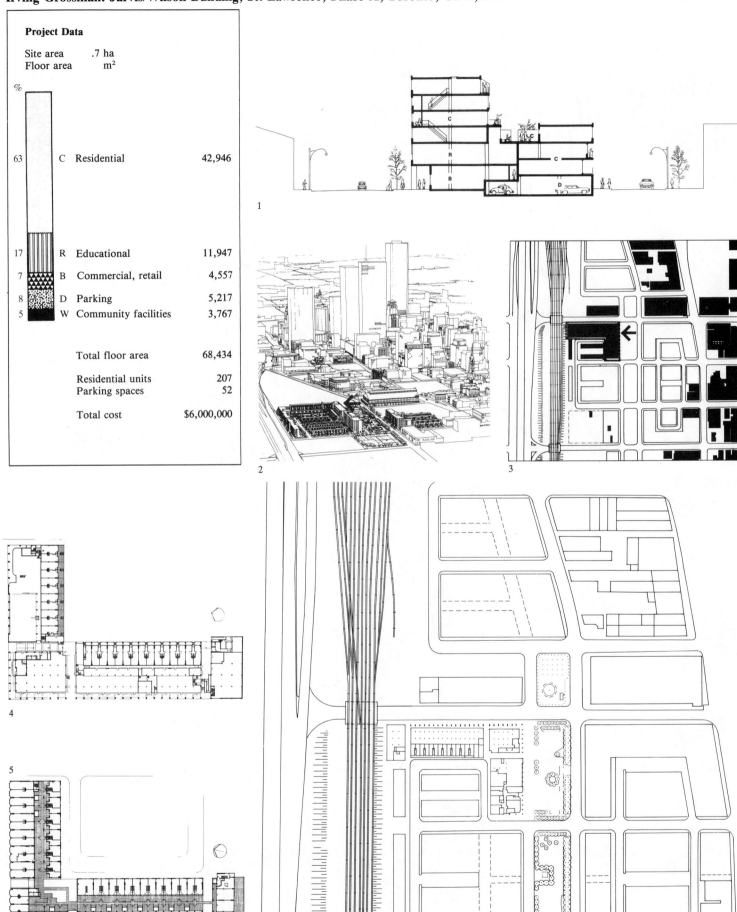

1

2

3

4

5

6

7

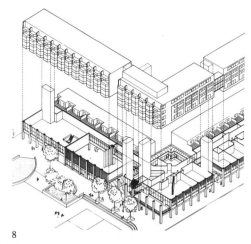

8

9

10

1 Section
2 Aerial perspective
3 Figure ground plan
4 Second floor plan
5 Third floor plan
6 Ground floor plan
7 View from Jarvis Street
8 Axonometric
9 Dwelling units above school
10 View of private terraces

Herman Hertzberger: Music Centre, Utrecht, NL, 1979

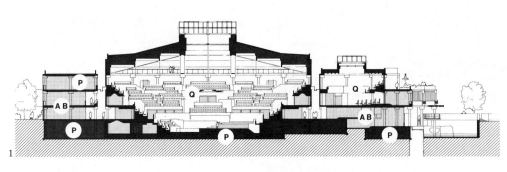

1

Project Data		
Site area	.8 ha	
Floor area	m²	

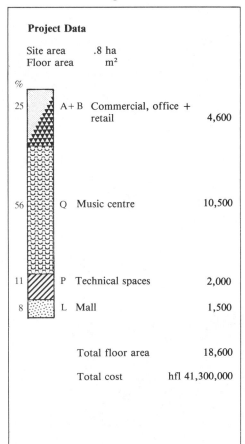

%				
25	A+B	Commercial, office + retail	4,600	
56	Q	Music centre	10,500	
11	P	Technical spaces	2,000	
8	L	Mall	1,500	
		Total floor area	18,600	
		Total cost	hfl 41,300,000	

1 Typical section
2 Figure ground plan
3 Site plan and ground floor plan
4 Perspective
5 Overall view of concert hall
6 View from upper buffet
7 Interior perspective
8 Large auditorium
9 View of concert hall
10 View of upper level

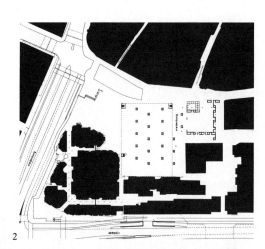

2

3

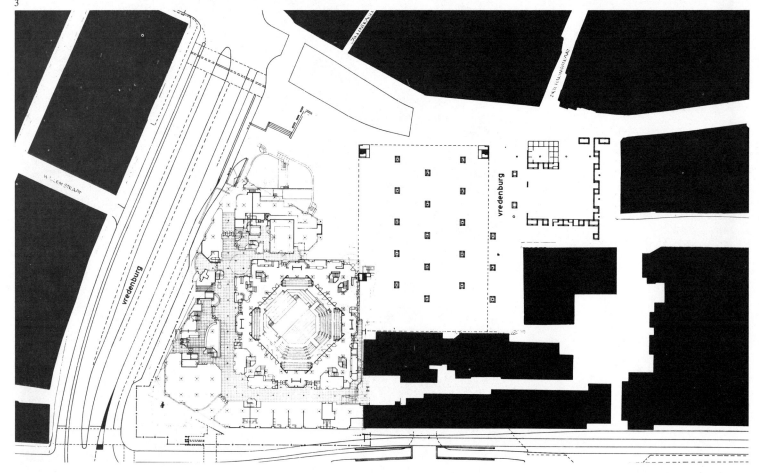

6

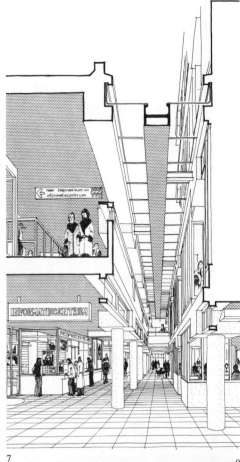

7

8

9

Zeidler Roberts Partnership: Queen's Quay Terminal, Toronto, CDN, 1980

Project Data
Site area   1.75 ha
Floor area   m²

%				m²
48	A	Commercial, office		34,280
23	B	Commercial, retail		16,572
19	C	Residential		13,749
8	D	Parking		5,406
2	V	Theater		1,625
		Total floor area		71,632
		Residential units		72
		Parking spaces		85

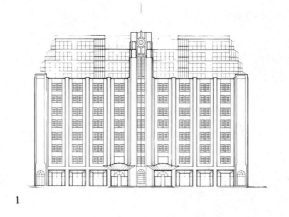

1

1   North elevation
2   Figure ground plan
3   Site plan and ground floor plan
4   North-South section
5   North-East elevation

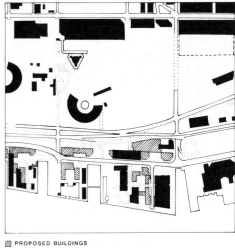

2

▨ PROPOSED BUILDINGS

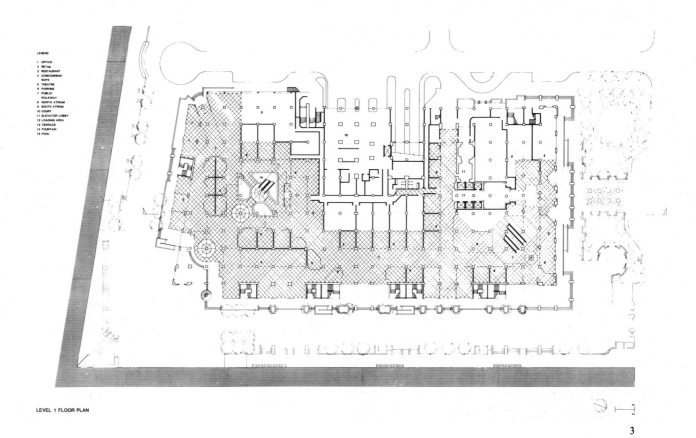

LEGEND

1 OFFICE
2 RETAIL
3 RESTAURANT
4 CONDOMINIUM SUITE
5 THEATRE
6 PARKING
7 PUBLIC WALKWAY
8 NORTH ATRIUM
9 SOUTH ATRIUM
10 COURT
11 ELEVATOR LOBBY
12 LOADING AREA
13 TERRACE
14 FOUNTAIN
15 POOL

LEVEL 1 FLOOR PLAN

3

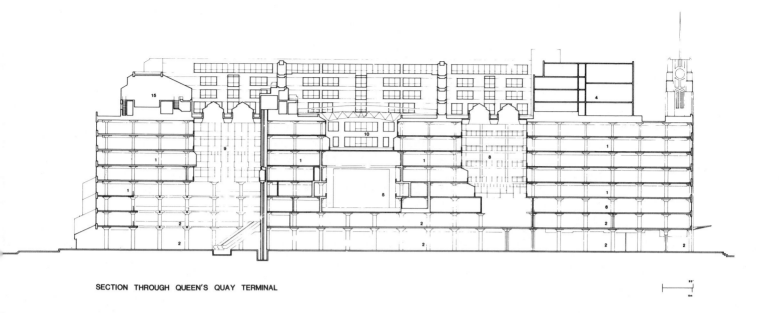

SECTION THROUGH QUEEN'S QUAY TERMINAL

QUEEN'S QUAY TERMINAL
TORONTO ONTARIO

ZEIDLER ROBERTS PARTNERSHIP
ARCHITECTS

4

5

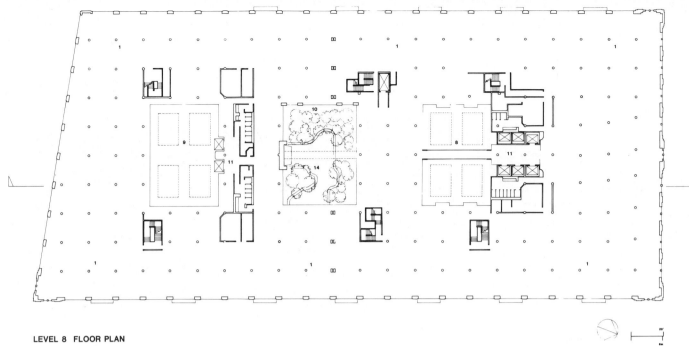

LEVEL 8 FLOOR PLAN

6

LEVEL II FLOOR PLAN

7

6 Typical office floor plan
7 Typical residential floor plan
8 Interior view of theatre
9 Southwest entrance
10 Southeast entrance
11 South atrium

8

94

9

10

11

Part III
The Multi-Use Building in the Urban Context

Historical Background

Rediscovery of Multi-Use Buildings

As discussed in Part I, multi-use buildings are not new, however they were deliberately banned from the vocabulary of modern architecture. The belief in functionalism's efficacy to solve urban problems, as expressed in the Athens Charter, was the official death knell of multi-use structures. The ultimate goal was to breed building types that fitted the function they should serve. Since each function, such as living, working, etc. is different, it seemed logical that their building containers had to be different and that the ideal container without compromising the efficiency of its function could only serve one single function. Modern architectural philosophy eventually influenced the bylaws and rules of most cities to such a degree that it became difficult, by law, to build a multi-use building.

Modern architects, assuming that a building's form ist mainly influenced by such functional needs, created design theories that demanded a prime status for functional requirements. They did not allow an equal status to other considerations such as response to cultural imprints or the integration within the urban fabric.

The isolated building prototypes developed by modern architecture – such as the apartment tower, the office tower, the shopping centre or the one-family house – may fulfill their internal demands; however, thoughtlessly pushed together, they cannot create a coherent city.

These prototypes create an isolated environment serving one function only. People will soon leave such district after having done the particular task. Apartment districts will be empty during the day and office districts will be abandoned after five o'clock. Modern city districts of such single-use buildings lack the complexity and life involvement that "old" city spaces still offer.

It is now our task to put these separated parts together so that their forms and activities complement each other and create again a vital urban life.

Restraints on Building Multi-Use Structures Today

Many of the examples shown in Part II have their problems. Often they show the struggle that still exists, not only to accept the concept of multi-use philosophically, but also to build it in a world that tries to prevent its existence through legislative, financial and operational restrictions.

For the last three years in the City of Toronto a heroic battle has been fought over the change of bylaws to permit multi-use buildings in its core. The major argument brought forward against this attempt has been that combining several functions within one building is uneconomic. Combining housing and commercial spaces was claimed to be not only economically wasteful from a construction viewpoint, but furthermore inefficient from an operational and management standpoint.

The statistics used in this argument, however only reflect the specialization of the construction industry as it is today. Over the years specialized building techniques have enabled economical construction of single-use buildings. We should not forget that the first prototypes of monofunctional buildings were not particularly efficient in light of today's expertise. Only repetition and refinement has created what financial streamlining now exists, but even then their economic benefits are questionable from an urban economic view when these buildings begin to occupy whole city districts to the detriment of the city.

Multi-use buildings could achieve equal or greater individual efficiency, but both building bylaws and financial attitudes are still against such multi-use. For example, most funding for housing in Canada is done through the Canadian Mortgage and Housing Corporation. It is difficult to obtain mortgaging from it for housing projects that have more than a ten per cent commercial component.

1
Ludwig Richter
The old multiuse building combining workplace and living into one structure

97

2

3

4

The argument that monofunctionalism is the natural developmental pattern is based on the assumption that single-use buildings supposedly achieve greater individual efficiencies. If we view this within the context of the city, we realize that such efficiency really does not exist. Single-use structures and their districts are occupied for only part of each day or week and stand empty and unused the rest of the time. Multi-use structures, however, bring people together at different times – a much more efficient use of urban space. Even the supposed economic savings of the individual single-use buildings do not hold up to scrutiny. Though multi-use buildings may initially cost more to construct, they are cheaper in the long run considering their more intensive use in the urban context.

Monofunctionalism, if left to grow uncontrolled, will ultimately destroy the life of a city and eventually, therefore, the individual building itself. New York's Bronx housing, the Pruitt Igoe housing in St. Louis, and Detroit's downtown office district are a few well-known examples that attest to this.

Multi-Use Versus Utopianism

The danger of Utopian concepts is that they try to rectify a known system by totally supplanting it with a new untried system. This usually leads to new problems that are often greater than those they tried to correct. Le Corbusier's vision of Ville Radieuse and Frank Lloyd Wright's Broad Acres both tried to resolve apparent problems by creating a new system that eradicated the old.

Even the partial realization of their concepts resulted in unanticipated problems that were many times more severe than the ones they tried to remedy. Le Corbusier thought he could create a new balance of life by segregating the functions of working and living, using the freedom that modern modes of transportation seemed to offer. He envisioned a residential environment filled with trees and sunshine far removed from the grime of industrial cities. Unfortunately, he did not realize that the new city, having new technologies and production methods would not need such segregation.

His segregation of function destroyed the symbiotic life that existed in the old city. The isolated office city created an environment of uniform consistency which lacked the variety necessary to a vibrant city. The other half of such a streamlined existence, the residential city, also failed. Both forced the totality of city life into a schizophrenic, unhealthy existence.

Reality usually prevents theories from running their full course, and also here prevented this concept from being totally realized. Many things helped to keep the fabric of the old cities alive, particularly in Europe. Paradoxically, the sense of tradition, neglected and even rejected by modern architectural philosophy, helped defeat attempts to "modernize" the old city completely. This sense of historicism kept the city's historical precedents alive as a cultural continuum from the past. The most successful urban spaces of today are paradoxically those that have used the historical precedent like Munich's pedestrian zone.

Multi-Use: Vital to Urban Symbiosis

At the beginning of this century modern town planning philosophies concerned only with a misunderstood functionalism were propounded. They took control in North American cities after the Second World War and created irreparable damage. The huge urban experiment of segregating functions nearly led to the demise of the American city. Jane Jacobs presented a penetrating description of the results in her book, "The Death and Life of Great American Cities."

The premise that multi-use buildings can help restore the city's health depends on our understanding of the complex interrelationships within a city. As in any living organism, so also in a city, an intricate dependence exists between its many parts. Sometimes such interdependencies are not immediately apparent in a healthy city, however they soon show up if any part is omitted.

Symbiosis, the interaction of different organisms for the benefit of all, also operates in a city. The physical proximity of different functions is of aid to each function involved. Bring people together for a night at the theatre and nearby restaurants get more business. Put retail stores near the restaurants and people who go into that area for the food will buy at the shops or attend the theatre, often simply because these functions are close to each other. On the other hand, remove all residences from an office district and at five o'clock that area becomes deserted and finally dangerous. It dies without the life-giving support of other city functions.

There are thousands of human beings in a city – each with a different lifestyle, each at a different stage of life, each with different interests, emotions, habits and relationships – they all need an urban environment that relates to their

2
Pickering, Ontario
Modern monofunctional shopping centre

3
Modern monofunctional apartment tower

4
Le Corbusier
La Ville Radieuse
Aerial view

5
Ed's warehouse
Successful symbiosis between restaurant and theater

6
Example of postmodern formalism: Venturi's Ionic column

7
Munich Pedestrian Zone

5

6

7

different physical needs. The city fabric must be rich and complex enough to properly fulfill these different needs and allow a beneficial, symbiotic interaction between them. Multi-use structures can provide the background environment, for such interaction.

Dangers of One-sided Formalism

We must not fall victim to the same mistake that limited modern architectural thought. It appeared to the fathers of modern architecture that their predecessors were steeped in historic eclecticism and were hiding the truth of modern technology. Having discovered this omission, they dogmatized their credo into the half truth that only through the faithful expression of function and technology a new architecture could be formed. We now find ourselves approaching a similar though reversed position. Seeing how modern architecture was preoccupied with functionalism and neglected the other forces that shape our environment, particularly those connected with human emotions and cultural heritage, the pendulum has now swung in the opposite direction.

Many examples of the so-called post-modern architecture appear to deny function and construction their rightful, even if not dominant, existence. We might easily slide again into a different formalism and fail to create a richer architecture. Architecture can only come to life if it fulfills all demands – those of function and construction as well as those of emotion.

Since the multi-use building is part of the city fabric, it therefore is subject to its rules. It is not sufficient to measure a building on individual benefits alone and forget the city from which it takes its life. Ultimately, not only the internal needs of the building, but also the external needs of the city must be contained within one building. Thus a building must compromise in order to become *one*.

I have chosen three stances from which to look at and evaluate the multi-use building as part of this greater urban whole:

1. *The forces that shape the multi-use building from within.*
In this context I will discuss the needs of the building as an individual complex – its inner functions, its responses to user needs, and the form that it will express through the characteristics of its structure. – enlarging on established principles of architecture, but looking at them in a different way.

2. *The response of the multi-use building to the demands of its external urban environment.*
Here I will investigate the conditions and rules of society as a whole within which the individual building exists and the concept of the building as an element of urban space.

3. *The physical expression of the multi-use building as a response to emotions.*
Here I will develop the proposition that emotions have an independent status in creating a building's form. Modern architecture, in its philosophical dogma, denied this force its independency and saw emotions only as an extension of functional and structural needs.

Modern architecture has been particularly insensitive towards any compromise that could result from integrating these three positions. For example, a building's façade was only acceptable to modern architects if it reflected internal function as the "inner truth" of the individual building. This was considered to be the only expression or compromise that should be reflected in its form. The other meaning of façade – namely compliance with the external urban context it stands in – was totally negated. A building's functions often change in a cyclic pattern during the life of that building. Perhaps there is as much relevance for the exterior of the building to relate to its urban environment than in expressing its inner truth.

This relation to the urban context is the second compromise that the multi-use building must reflect in its architectural form. Otherwise, it could neither participate in nor contribute to its city.

Finally, we must accede to the third compromise required of the multi-use building: that emotional needs, related to cultural heritage and human psychology, act independently from internal and external needs in shaping our buildings.

The façade is only one part in which we see these three issues reflected. We must investigate and understand how the multi-use building should respond to these and how it can compromise between them to rehabilitate our urban fabric.

Adelaide Park Apartments – Zeidler Roberts Partnership/Architects

Such a seemingly naive yet effective response to the downtown street as street-related retail and living space above was refuted in modern planning theories. They are just being rediscovered in conjunction with the continuous street façade.

This building was the test case of the new Toronto downtown by-law that allowed housing again in the city core and prescribed a continuous height for buildings enclosing St. James Cathedral and its park. The façade here in its tripartite division responded as a space enclosure creating rhythm through the superimposition of two scales.

8a
Ground floor plan

8b
Typical floor plan

8c
Perspective view from park

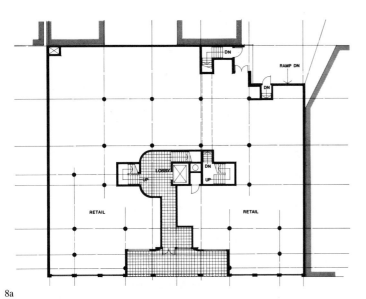

8a

8b

8c

100

8d
View of south elevation from park

8e
View east

8d

8e

101

Forces that Shape Multi-Use Structures

Internal Demands
Key Functions

In the last half century we have attempted to separate the various functions of human life from each other to improve their efficiency. However we have come to realize that in this process of separation we lost some of the most important qualities of urban life, namely the richness that lies in its complexity and contrast. To regain this loss it is not enough to just put these functions together again, without first to investigate these key activities of human life – work, recreation, inhabitation – alone and then in interaction with each other in order to understand how they can be integrated within the multi-use building.

Before examining the above three functions in more detail, we should first discuss what happens when these functions are isolated from each other in an urban environment, as was advocated and brought about by modern city planners.

Segregation of Function

The danger inherent in any new planning theory is that the concepts they introduce are often followed too literally. New theories are frequently only reactions to old ones and try to rectify previous mistakes. A prime example is the segregation of function. CIAM tried to correct the urban problems of the industrial city by segregating those functions that seemed to interfere with each other, however, their cure became worse than the original malady.

In our current attempt to bring back a multi-use city we must be careful not to overreact in the opposite direction and exclude all segregation of functions. There exists a level of segregation at which an individual function reaches its optimum potential. Nobody will disagree that a factory with obnoxious fumes or noises is harmful to a residential area and should be segregated, however, this is no reason for all work places to be banned from residential districts.

The CIAM's over-emphasis on separating functions was a major cause in eliminating multi-use buildings from our cities. Yet the apparent confusion they were trying to eliminate is essential for a vibrant, healthy city. The experience of the last decades has clearly shown that such segregation leads ultimately to a city's stagnation. Nevertheless, totally eliminating segregation is not the answer either. Each function improves when segregated to a certain level, but it also requires a close interaction with other functions beyond this level in order to maintain its vibrancy.

Therefore, my thesis is that this level of segregation in most cases should not be carried out in city districts, an action which creates single-use areas lacking urban interaction, rather this should be done within the building itself, letting different functions cohabitate in it. Such cohabitation not only creates satisfactory conditions for individual functions, but through the phenomenon of symbiosis creates urban action that is greater than the sum of its isolated parts. This is the *raison d'être* of the multi-use structure.

The isolation of residential activities into districts (i. e. bedroom cities), thought to be beneficial in making a healthier environment, actually produced detrimental side-effects. The elimination of all places of work from the residen-

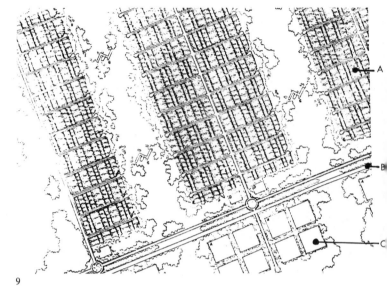

9

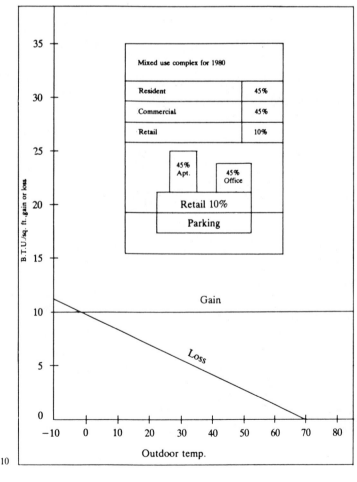

9
L. Hilberseimer (1944)
Utopian reorganization of the big city based on functional segregation
A   Residential
B   Highway
C   Factories

10
Heat gain and loss

10

11

12

tial suburbs created a society where most males were present only on weekends. This also took potential customers away from suburban areas during the day and made it difficult for many commercial activities, such as small restaurants, pubs, specialty stores, etc., to survive economically. Thus other social activities in such neighbourhoods were reduced even further, which encouraged finally the functional isolation of the new, regional shopping mart.

Examples of this functional isolation reach everywhere into the fabric of our life and cities. Toronto, for instance, once had an old, small city zoo. It was a Victorian-picture-book one, where bears sat in cages and children stuck lollipops between the bars at them. The zoo, in the heart of downtown, was full of people at all times of the day, but was rather shabby. You would see young mothers there, pushing baby carts from the nearby apartments, chatting with friends while their children were awed by the antics of monkeys.

Unfortunately, progress and civic pride demanded a better zoo. Instead of using the downtown ravine lands, a large tract of ground outside the city was chosen; an hour's travel by highway from downtown and with no primary public transit connection. The organizers of this magnificent facility are now amazed at the relative under-use of their isolated zoo. Of course, it has become a tourist attraction, a theme park that people go to as a planned activity; if they have a car and enough money for parking and admission, and have a whole day to spend. But the zoo has lost its function as a vibrant urban place and it is this loss which saddens.

Concentration of Function

There are advantages to a certain concentration of a function within a small area. To a degree the isolation of a function helps achieve efficiency. This, however, does not contradict that ultimate isolation achieves the opposite. An excellent example of the useful concentration of one function could be found in the Medieval city where certain trades took over certain streets. One street would be occupied mainly by shoemakers, another by goldsmiths, etc. Such inner-professional competition improved the guilds, the product, and offered the customer an easily accessible choice. This is still true in cities today. Sometimes certain activities search each other out and reinforce each other, as witnessed in the streets of specialty boutiques found in many cities.

Theatres, too, have often concentrated in certain districts, but never to the exclusion of other amenities to social life. Only modern planning brought about the isolated cultural complex, exemplified by the Lincoln Centre in New York. The simple fact that it is impossible for an individual to visit two performances in one evening was overlooked. Thus, the geographic adjacency of opera house and theatre has little usefulness and even less sense to it.

Easy access, ample parking, a choice of restaurants, and a pleasant environment to enjoy both before and after the theatre are essential to the pleasure of theatre-going. Where several theatres are scattered about in one area, they can all partake of and reinforce the existence of the same benefits without choking each other to death and still allow urban life at non-performance times.

Specialization of Function

The internal needs for the shelter of human activities have become more complex over the centuries and more specialized towards particular requirements. Such specialization and adaptation to function are necessary for the evolutionary development of any living organism. They enable more effective solutions to be found to problems, and allow progressively a more efficient use of the environment.

However, specialization in itself does not represent progress. We must realize that specialization not only spells evolution, it can also bring about extinction. Specialization harbours two fatal flaws. First, in the beginning it allows a species to use its environment more efficiently, thus encouraging a growth of the species which later leads to overcrowding. This then abuses the environment by depleting the factor that is over-used, which in turn leads to the decimation of species. Second, specialization renders a species unable to cope with or adapt quickly to such changed environment.

Our ability to live in huge social conglomerations is the result of specialization; yet we must be careful not to extend this too far and become subject to its negative influences. Many of the faults of modern cities can be traced back to over-specialization. Particularly the North American core cities specialized in commercial uses and the resultant deterioration of them is only one of many examples.

The city's life will be improved by encouraging a cross-relation of diverse functions, not only within each district but also within multi-use buildings. Such

11	12
New York specialty shopping. Orchard Street district	Lincoln Center, New York Isolated cultural function

Trinity Square Development – Zeidler Roberts Partnership/Architects

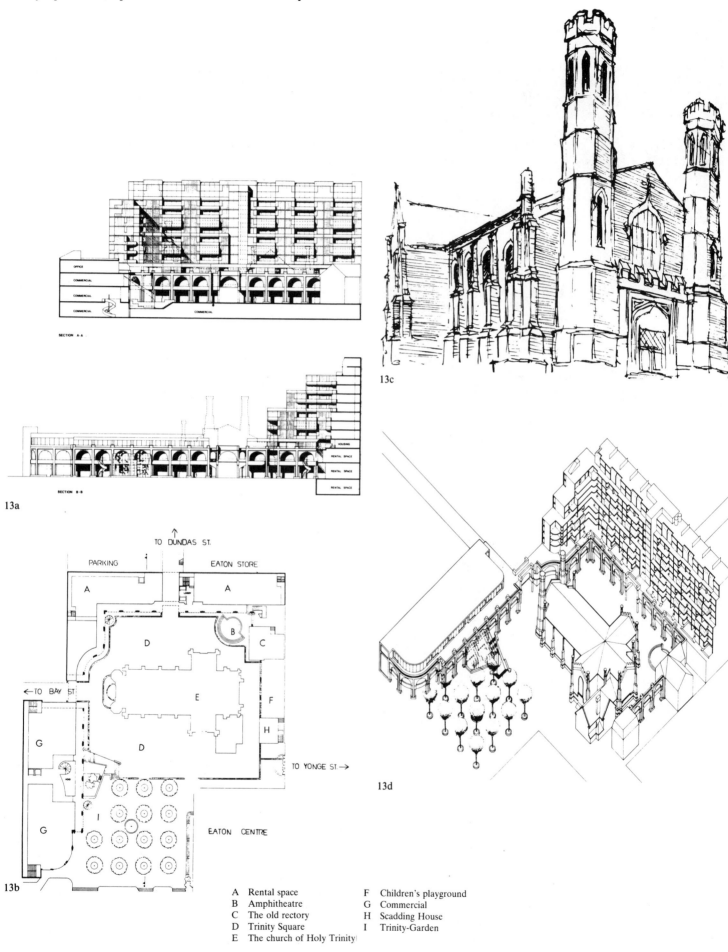

13a

13b

13c

13d

A Rental space
B Amphitheatre
C The old rectory
D Trinity Square
E The church of Holy Trinity

F Children's playground
G Commercial
H Scadding House
I Trinity-Garden

The project is an attempt to revitalize the landlocked space around the Church of the Holy Trinity between the Eaton Centre, the Eaton store and the Bell Telephone Centre and further to transpose it through arcaded retail stores into a lively square with artist's studios, offices and apartments above.

The architectural accentuation of the two-storied arcade, which is kept just below the eave line of the church, serves to give back to the Holy Trinity its original visual predominance, as seen from the perspective of a pedestrian. The apartment building shields the blank fire wall of the existing Eaton store. However, because it is set back, it does not detract from the visual importance of the arcade. The west façade of the Eaton Centre has also been stepped down to visually emphasize the importance of the old church.

13e

13f

13a
Sections looking north and west

13b
Ground floor plan

13c
Trinity Church

13d
Axonometric of Trinity Square

13e
View of Trinity Square looking west

13f
View of garden and church looking north

14

15

16

cross-relation should be designed to allow people and their activities the benefits of interaction without losing the advantages inherent in specialization.

Inhabitation
Historical Development

Very early in the development of the city came the need to protect the life and enterprise of its citizens. This need led to the gathering together of the inhabitants and their varying activities within the walls of the city.

While this did not always produce optimum living conditions, especially in European towns of the Middle Ages, the Medieval city created urban forms, for which we have acquired an emotional affinity. In many cases Medieval cities work still better than their sanitized modern counterparts. The crowded living conditions, narrow yards and limited private spaces are not as unsatisfactory as was assumed. The compactness and richness of this environment afforded great choice to the citizens. Especially pleasing was the abrupt juxtaposition of urban space with open landscape that offered two alternate environments within walking distance of one another.

The industrial city changed this situation drastically. The city's growing size increased. Overcrowding and the interference of incompatible activities within it created ghastly living conditions for most. Ebenezer Howard's Garden City, the German Siedlungen, and similar architectural models became the ideal to be pursued in search of a solution.

With railroads and streetcars there came not only a greater concentration of populations in cities, but also the possibility of greater diversification and segregation. A man's place of work and place of living no longer had to coincide. With such an arrangement it was assumed that optimum residential conditions could again be obtained. Privacy, sun, places for children to play – all these appeared to be possible without having to arrest the growth of the city.

Let us examine some aspects of urban life and habitation affected by the architectural planning theories that have proliferated since the industrial revolution.

Loss of Urban Life

Modern planning theories led to a tripartite view of the city – inhabitation, work, recreation – with the expectation that optimum results would be achieved if each function could develop in zoned districts.

The physical manifestations of these theories have not fulfilled their promise. Something was wrong with these assumptions.

The segregation of living accommodation and work place sacrificed an urban life style and the freedom of choice it offered.

We are now realizing that to maintain a vibrant city life we must mix again its various uses and activities on as small a scale as possible, without ignoring the individual needs of each use. This should be done at a level that relates to the individual human being. We must investigate how human habitat can be integrated into the multi-use building. This should include not only the physical *living forms* that can be created within such confines, but also the potential *living style* that can be offered through such cross-relation with other key functions.

Human Adaptability

Studies done to establish parameters for ideal living conditions are nearly countless; and so are the possible solutions. Modern architecture's hope of creating the perfect prototype living unit has not been realized. Neither have standards or regulations achieved better living conditions, nor really prevented bad ones. Therefore, I feel little can be gained by discussing in detail the physical design of the unit itself. However, it is important to discuss the relation of a unit within a multi-use complex.

Man is adaptable to many different living conditions. He can still live happily in houses built hundreds of years ago. He can also be equally happy in versions

14
Rothenburg o. T.
Walled medieval town. Juxtaposition of town versus country

15
Industrial city. Overcrowding

16
Tony Garnier (1869–1948)
Cité Industrielle
Perspective of residential area

of space-age visions. Shelter for human beings can take many forms. Between the nomad tent and the New York penthouse lies a wide range of variants. Even though people live in habitational extremes, each will think he has found the best living conditions for himself (if it was his choice); and he may have, because the same answer is not right for everyone.

Human happiness is not completely a result of outside forces, for it arises from within the mind of the individual. Yet neither is happiness totally divorced from environment, no matter *how* adaptable an individual is.

Home: An Emotional State

Man can live pretty well anywhere and be content, yet he is most content in a physical environment he conceives as home, with all its attendant emotional overtones, which relate among others to inherited social and cultural attitudes. These attitudes differ from culture to culture.

In Victorian England, for example, a front parlour was essential to a certain life style. This parlour was kept long after its need vanished, for it had become an indicator of social status.

Here in Toronto inherited social mores have also dictated the form the home took, shaping its interior in ways often contrary to logic. Toronto's residential areas are graced by beautiful treed ravines that carry small tributaries into the main rivers. The houses built during the 1920's on lots bordering these ravines ignored the natural beauty of their sites in order to follow social convention. Major rooms and windows faced the street. The rugged beauty of the ravine could only be seen through small bathroom or kitchen apertures. However, these sought-after ravine homes are now being remodelled, and the floor plans turned around to take advantage of their magnificent views.

But even today social conventions are carried to similar absurdities. In North America especially, attempts to provide social status require that backyard patios and Georgian manor porticoes be placed where they neither fit nor make sense.

Such socio-cultural attitudes should not merely be thought of as manifestations of immaturity. They require serious consideration since they influence our physical spaces, even though time and physical realities eventually change these attitudes.

The large pioneer family of North America slowly changed into the nuclear family, and homes diminished in size. The functions carried on inside homes also altered. Today, even though marriage and the role of woman in society are changing rapidly, with a resultant change in the home's actual function, society's emotional response to the idea of home lingers in the past. This dichotomy between the present reality and the emotional milieu which lags in the past is expressed in our approach to housing.

This dichotomy has created the subculture of the "spec" house that follows its own aesthetic rules – rules which are quite different from the codes of the ruling high art of modernism. This "spec art", like folk art, adapts its forms from the past and its function from the present. Georgian detail on the modern bungalow is an example of such emotional attachment to the past. The emotional recall of past forms that seems to dictate the post-modern form world of today is a partial acceptance of these forces which are latent in our society.

The form of a home is not solely developed through the expression of its functions, nor can its beauty be deducted from this basis alone. Both cultural-historical precedent and social-psychological imprint strongly influence what we want in our environment. Indeed, there is no incongruity in seeing "Canadiana" pine furniture in a penthouse apartment. It acts like a mental security blanket for its owner, and helps hide the reality of being perched on a concrete cliff twenty stories above a roaring metropolis. Habitat must answer man's need for a home which relates to his emotional and cultural heritage.

17
Nomad tent

18
New York penthouse

19
E. H. Zeidler
Beaumont House
1917 house adjusted to ravine setting

20

21

22

The Living Unit in the Urban Context

The relationship of the living unit to its urban environment has been neglected. In order to better understand this interrelation, let us look at aspects which must be considered if we want to integrate living units into the urban context: the domicile's relationship:
a) to physical conditions,
b) to its social environment,
c) to urban density, and,
d) to and integration with key functions.

a) The Domicile's Relationship to Physical Conditions
Changing Physical Requirements

A person has different needs at different stages in his life, just as different people have different needs. A single person, living alone or with friends, requires other things from a home than does a couple with small children. Some people spend most of their lives in their homes; some mostly away from their homes. A living unit's relationship to the environment is particularly important if the person has to spend much time within it. If he just comes home to sleep then perhaps only a few things matter, such as noise and ventilation. But a mother with young children who spends most of her time at home is much more affected by such things as the relationship to the ground, outdoor playing space, view, penetration of sun, shade, ventilation, and so on. It is, therefore, nearly impossible to establish meaningful physical parameters beyond some obvious generalities, and codes that have attempted to be specific have only succeeded in eliminating a variety of choices. For example, quite successful living unit layouts in Europe are not possible in North America and vice versa because of such well-meaning code restrictions.

House versus Apartment

There is usually a dichotomy between what a person wants as a home and the environment he actually ends up living in. In a recent study of housing needs and expectations for a community of 14000, we found that despite a wide range in age, social background and family status, most people wanted a single family dwelling. It was only when economic factors were taken into account that other forms of housing were considered. Living in an urban environment is, of course, an economic consideration.

Many people don't like living in apartments, even though apartments are the major form of urban housing in existence. Perhaps one of the major drawbacks is the lack of semi-public space, a function fulfilled by the front porch and lawn in the North American house. This type of house in the past was both private and social – it gave spaces for solitude and for social intercourse. Its front porch was a semi-public space where a person could be on his own ground, yet at the same time could look for social contact. In modern apartment living forms such "in between" spaces have been forgotten, creating a serious deficiency. Nobody will be found on a rocking chair in his apartment corridor for any length of time before being carried away.

Multi-use buildings must exploit fully the relationship of living unit with its immediate environment. The possibilities are only limited by imagination, yet very little has been done to create desirable urban housing. Apartment towers, thoughtlessly planned, still dominate our urban landscape despite the longing for a home by most of its inhabitants.

Downtown Housing in Peril

The modern city should offer a choice of living options, including housing in the downtown. This allows a life style that appeals to many. However, downtown housing does something else too – it creates life in the downtown and extends its activities. More importantly, it can bring back a sense of security to the nearly abandoned city core of many American cities.

Unfortunately, housing will not simply move into downtown on its own. Conditions must be created that encourage such a move. A major obstacle to downtown housing is the high cost of land. When both commercial and residential uses are permitted by the municipality, the developer will likely choose commercial as it is more profitable. Only when the ratio of commercial to residential use is fixed by zoning bylaws will the latter be built to any extent.

20
"Spec art." Georgian detail on the modern bungalow

21
Front porch of the North American house as the rudiment of a semipublic space

22
St. James, Toronto
Thoughtlessly planned apartment tower

23

24

b) The Domicile's Relationship with its Social Environment
Social Integration

Economics have dictated the building of large numbers of nearly uniform housing units. This, in turn, has resulted in socio-economic groupings becoming concentrated in one area, forming ghettos, either for the poor or the rich.

Much social unrest in the past few decades can be traced back to the concentration of such socially segregated groups. Thus, it is obviously preferable to have a mixture of people belonging to various socio-economic groups live in any one area.

A viable grouping, however, cannot be achieved by merely mixing individuals with differing social and economic backgrounds. People still prefer having a neighbour with social habits similar to their own. Within a small space, such as the immediate street neighbourhood, a certain homogeny is preferable. Yet segregation should not extend much beyond this scale; such small areas must be integrated with different social groupings to prevent the formation of ghettos.

For example, the North American practice of building student housing often has isolated thousands of students from the rest of the city. Such a social environment is bound to create student attitudes that the rest of their community sees as being unrealistic, and vice versa. When groups are intermixed, members of each group will understand more readily the problems of the others. This prevents any group from assuming that its problems are the only real ones.

I am aware that it is difficult to maintain such social complexity in an urban district even if one could introduce it in the beginning. There seems to be a social force at work that attempts to make a district homogeneous, even if it was originally heterogeneous; and this is particulary true in districts that lack a flexibility in building forms.

However, a district of great physical complexity can better maintain its social complexity than one of physical uniformity. For example, the Donvale area in Toronto has a great variety of housing forms and has maintained, if not increased, its social complexity despite changes that threatened to convert the district from a working-class area into a middle-class neighbourhood.

c) The Domicile's Relationship to Urban Density

By its very nature, the multi-use building depends on density to be effective, although too high a density could limit this effectiveness.

Three inseparable key factors determine desirability of human habitat – quality of the physical environment, location or social context, and density. Not only is it impossible to measure them in absolute terms, but the presence of one affects the others.

Quality of Physical Environment

The desirability of urban residential areas is strongly influenced by the quality of the physical environment, whether that quality is real or imagined. We cannot establish scientifically measurable rules that assess this quality. People give different values to different urban environments, and the same environment may be valued differently at various times by the same people. Obviously in such assessments we move quickly from an objective, rational evaluation into a subjective, emotional one that is controlled by individual preferences and cultural codes. The situation is further complicated by social attitudes.

Social Context

Physical environments of nearly equal quality may become desirable or totally undesirable because of social shifts within the life cycle of a city. Beautiful residential areas have turned into slums, even though initially their physical qualities had not changed. The reverse has also happened where slum areas have become desirable districts with no major physical changes having been made to the "statistical" quality of their environments. Neither the density nor the physical shell itself were changed; what changed was the social attitude which eventually altered the physical shell's appearance.

23
Levittown ghetto

24
Don Vale District, Toronto
Physical complexity permits relative
social complexity

Harbour City 1970

25a

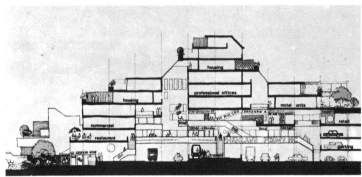

25b

25c

Harbour City was the master plan for a community of 60,000 people on 735 acres of islands created through land fill on water lots at the foot of downtown Toronto. The various islands are linked by both roadways and public transportation to downtown Toronto. Each island will have a public transportation stop integrated with its chief commercial area.

Parking will be provided inside these blocks. No resident will be more than five minutes walk from access to the public transportation. Canals for boating, skating and scenic enjoyment will lace a typical island, in addition major canals and waterways between the islands will provide lagoons and regatta courses.

Three Basic Building Groups are Envisaged

1. *Transit stop centre:* These are high density mixed-use buildings containing all urban facilities including office, retail, housing, parking etc.
2. *Horizontal apartments:* These are walk up high density residential buildings, organized around a central street and a "horizontal" elevator that is tied into the intermediate public transportation system. These buildings could have other uses such as workshops, too. The horizontal apartment fingers are arranged approximately 600 feet apart from the next finger or housing unit, allowing each living unit view and privacy on one side, while on the other side, immediately connected to dense urban activities.
3. *Town House Clusters:* These are intermediate density residential buildings, designed to provide for private space and public space in immediate adjacency. The overall density planned is for 80 to 90 persons per acre, without using highrise construction. The density in the city of Toronto is 32 persons per acre.

A structural system was devised that would accommodate these diverse planning requirements and the various anticipated uses, as well as allowing for growth and change.

25a Exterior view	25d Harbour City in winter
25b Section	25e Aerial photo of Toronto
25c View from lake	25f Model of site

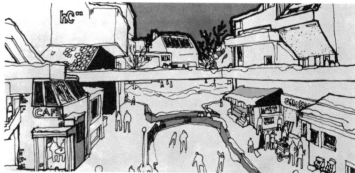

25d

25e

25f

St. Lawrence Housing T.T.C. Site

This site is a 2.5 acre city block with a 19th century industrial building at its north west corner that has been converted into a theatre. The programme includes 310 rental housing units ranging from town houses to various apartment types, 20,000 square feet of street, related retail, and a public library. The library court is connected with the esplanade by a pedestrian mews. All family units have their entrances from this pedestrian mews creating an active yet protected play area for children.

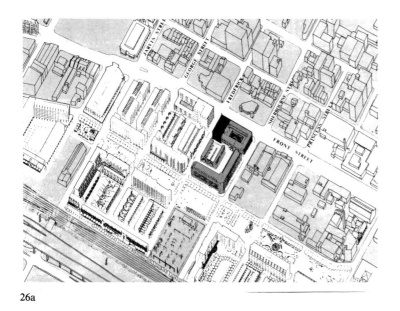

26a

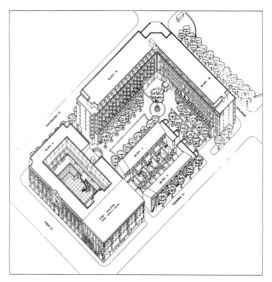

26b

26c

26a
Building in context

26b
Isometry

26c
Sherbourne Street elevation

University of Alberta Health Sciences Centre 1976–1985

This complex is a later application of this principle in a more urban situation. The individual buildings create protected interior streets that accommodate the more public functions, an urban solution particularly appropriate in severe climatic conditions.

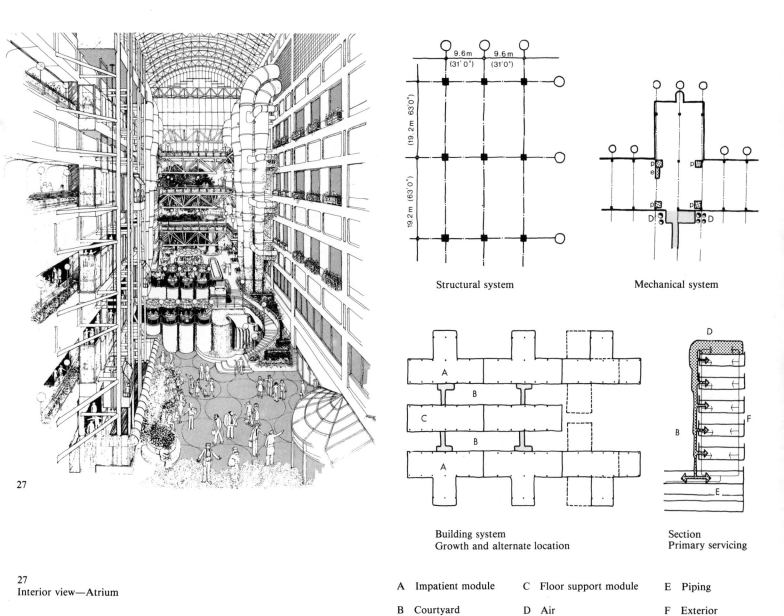

27

Structural system

Mechanical system

Building system
Growth and alternate location

Section
Primary servicing

27
Interior view—Atrium

A Impatient module   C Floor support module   E Piping

B Courtyard   D Air   F Exterior

113

28a

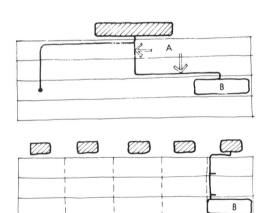

28b

Conventional central penthouse
air system

A Magnitude of work affected

B Modifications

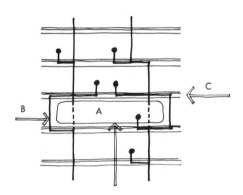

A Modification

B Vertical piping must be
   rerouted to accommodate
   change

C Ceiling

D Interstitial space

Conventional vertical custom-made
service

Unitized air system
Change not possible without
affecting all floors

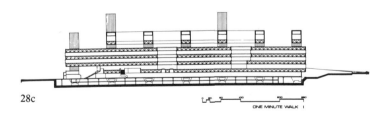

28c

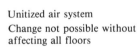
ONE MINUTE WALK

No disruption of levels above and below

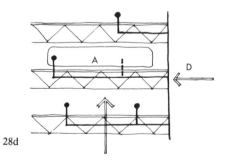

28d

Rationalized horizontal distribution
of mechanical services

This building was perhaps the first obsolescence-proof hospital; in other words, a structure whose shell could accommodate the everchanging activities of a hospital during its various life cycles.

The servo-system that was developed divided all elements of a conventional building into two categories: the Primary Elements, which do not change in the life of a hospital, and the Secondary Elements which must be changed when the use of a space is altered. The retention factor chart (32 f) indicates the percentage of these primary building elements that could become "constant" investments in the life cycle costs. As shown, the total percentage is 60% during any major change of function, while the maximum retention figure in a conventional building would be only 10% or less.

The two major elements that help to create such retention are the interstitial truss and the unitized air handling system.

Approximately 15% of the building cost is consumed by the structural system. At McMaster, we tried to create a structural system that would be able to accommodate any functional use without adjustments. We found that a 73.5 foot span (32 h) bridged by a truss was economically viable (32 g) and gave the planning freedom required. It also created the interstitial space needed to allow accessibility to the mechanical system (32 d).

The use of a unitized air system in conjunction with a predesigned distribution system also allowed the separation of the mechanical system into a constant primary system and a secondary system which minimizes the area affected by future changes (32 b). The result is a common building shell that contains within itself a variety of mixed uses ranging from such diverse functions as animal quarters, manufacturing areas, residential and office uses to complex medical facilities. The structure is capable of permitting the change into any of these functions in the future as required.

The principle is applicable in urban situations where activities are subject to changing life cycles yet individual buildings have an inherent investment that outlasts the initial function.

28a
Part of "Ring Street" adjacent to courtyard

28b
Unitized air system

28c
Section

28d
Interstitial space concept

28e
Exterior of McMaster

28e

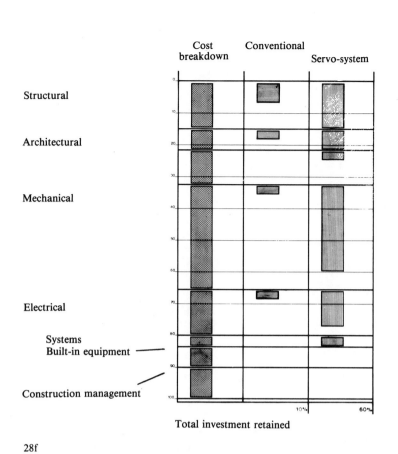

Structural

Architectural

Mechanical

Electrical

Systems
Built-in equipment

Construction management

Cost breakdown   Conventional   Servo-system

Total investment retained

28f

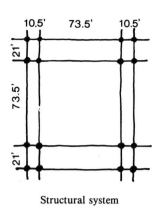

Structural system

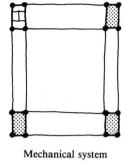

Mechanical system
Air, piping, and electrical combined

Building system
Incremental growth

28h

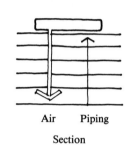

Air   Piping

Section

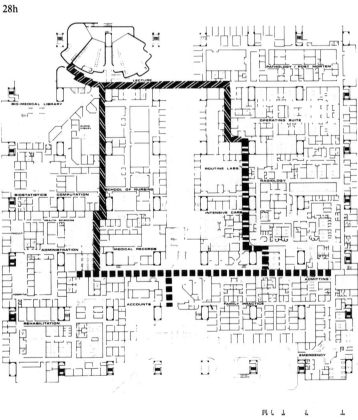

28g

Total structural cost per sq. ft. of floor area

Steel beams

8′ deep steel truss

Bay Size

(1 ft. = 0,3 m)

28i

■■■ In-patient traffic
■■▮ Out-patient traffic
▨▨▨ Student traffic

116

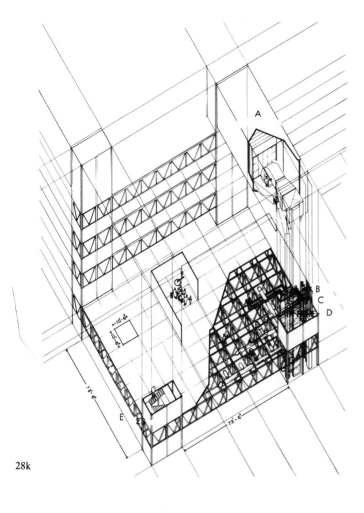

28k

A Mechanical air handling units
B Electric
C Plumbing
D Fume ducts
E Fire stair

28l

28f
Retention factor chart

28g
Total structural cost per sq. ft. of floor
area

28h
Systems diagram

28i
Traffic diagram

28k
"Servo-system"

28l
View of courtyard

Pickering Town Centre – 1977

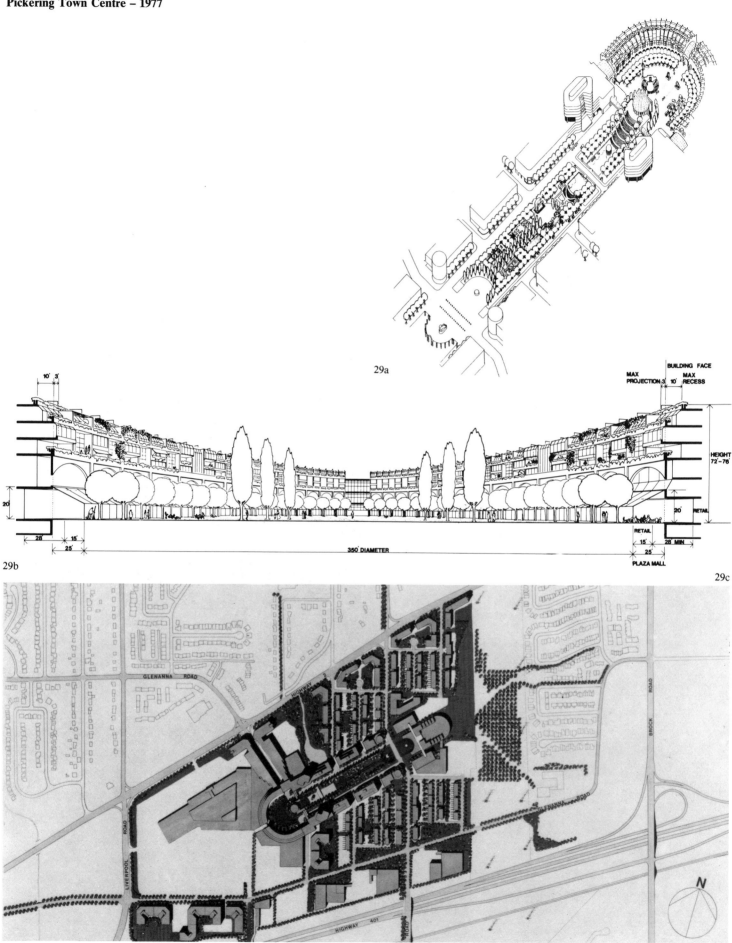

29a

29b

29c

1. *To establish a town form through urban design guide lines*
Conventional zoning determines allowable building volumes on a parcel by parcel basis. At Pickering a series of urban design controls for the entire site ensure the realization of a complete town form which can be developed gradually over time, according to these rules. In this way, the town is viewed as a collective entity with desired qualities, rather than a number of abstract undetermined sites.

2. *To ensure a structure for town growth through a street system and trees*
The problem of large areas of surface parking in the early years (a necessary consequence of inexpensive land) is turned into an opportunity. A basic structure of raised walkways and planting is used to subdivide the parking as well as to determine the ultimate pattern of streets and public spaces. This 'structure' for town growth is established at the outset of construction and gives the town an immediately recognizable topography.

3. *To reaffirm the value of the traditional street and its mixed use activities*
The Pickering proposal is based on familiar town elements: street, lane, plaza and civic park (the Esplande). A range of overlapping activities are supported by this basic structure. They include shops, offices, housing, community cultural and recreational spaces, transit facilities, department stores, schools and a hotel that are permitted o grow in a 'mixed' zoning plan.

29a
Main plaza and Esplanade Park

29c
Siteplan

29b
Section/perspective through main plaza

29d
Aerial view looking south

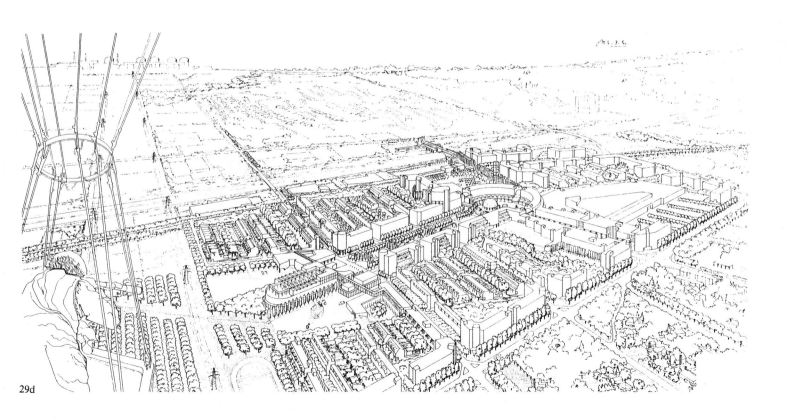

29d

30
Nob Hill, San Francisco

Density

It is wrong to assume that density is good or bad in itself. Contrary to the assumption that low density creates better living conditions, some of the most dense living quarters in large cities are often the most desirable ones, like Brooklyn Heights in New York or Nob Hill in San Francisco, as Jane Jacobs has pointed out.

Yet statistics alone mean nothing, because some of the worst urban slum areas also have similarly high densities.

Density is related to both the quality of the physical environment and the social context. Attempts to rebuild slums at lesser densities, even with a better physical environment (at least in terms of statistics), have seldom been successful unless they also dealt with the social context. For example, if density – which is necessary to bring urban amenities such as transportation, recreation and work within immediate contact of the habitat – is lowered, the district may no longer be economically able to support these facilities. This, in turn, would worsen the social context and ultimately the quality of the physical environment.

However, it is not necessary nor desirable in a metropolis to have large areas with equally high population densities. Despite these large concentrated densities, the overall population density in the total metropolitan area is relatively low due to improper usage of the urban area.

It would be better if land usage plans would be devised that encourage the super-concentration of density in smaller areas with the intervening release of lower density and open space. This would help to create a better quality in the physical environment without losing the transportation and economic viability of the district as a whole. Such arrangements of higher and lower densities intermixed allow greater options in the design of living units and their external relation to open space than the present planning attitude of spreading density over large areas equally like peanut butter.

d) The Domicile's Relationship to and Integration with Key Functions
Functions need Spacial Adjacency

A healthy city needs not only a mix of people but also a mix of activities. These must include active as well as passive ones. Children, adolescents, young couples, the elderly – all have different communal needs. In addition, various social groups demand different social stimulations. Communal activities should be closely interwoven with other facilities such as shops, restaurants, recreational spaces and places of work.

Limited thought has been given to combining the urban commercial street, high-density apartments and medium-density townhouses in one area. Such arrangements can create an environment in which most urban demands find their optimum fulfillment, where all necessary conditions – light, view, effective social density, public and private space, closeness to transportation, access to public parks etc. – can be achieved.

In such integrated designs, one function can borrow from another. The townhouse can live close to the high–rises' greater density and concomitant amenities without suffering from an increase of its own density. Conversely, the high-rise can take advantage of its proximity to the lower buildings and can use the view over the townhouses without being crowded and boxed in by neighbouring high-rises. The commercial street would not only be kept alive by all the people in the area, but would grow and expand, giving new life to the district. Within such an urban design, a richly varied social habitat can be created that is not limited to a single socio-economic group.

Another possibility to enrich city life is to take advantage of urban rooftops. Infrequent use has been made of the roofscapes created by large commercial functions. These spaces, for example, could be suitable for housing. By such multi-use, amenities can be created that benefit from the urban density. The roof garden at Montreal's Place Bonaventure and the planned apartments on top of Toronto's Eaton Centre and Trinity Square are examples. The multi-use building can make good use of the advantages offered by such urban conditions.

Transportation equals Functional Adjacency

Urban life creates freedom of choice through the closeness and variety of many activities. This freedom of choice relates to all phases of urban activities: the choice of having a wide variety of job opportunities without having to move one's domicile, the choice of living in different neighbourhoods without having to leave the city and last but not least to be able to participate in a rich and varied recreational and entertainment life that only the large urban centre can offer.

31

32

But the ability to make use of the choices is also related to mobility within the city. Thus transportation must be part of any urban planning. The failure of much North American planning since World War II has been due to the mistaken belief that cars alone could provide this needed mobility. The limits of this approach have become painfully obvious.

Cars and their insatiable need for space destroy the density that a city needs to unfold its urban life. Such density is not only needed to create urban activities but also to allow other transportation systems to develop.

Ideally, the stops along bus and streetcar routes should be no more than two to three minutes' walk from the point of origin or destination. Any distance taking more than five minutes' walk is too great and the use of such public transit systems will diminish if it is in competition with the car. This indicates also that transportation, particularly public transit, must relate to housing and commercial activities in order to achieve optimum integration of all functions. This ability of transportation to substitute for physical adjacency has led in modern planning to the mistaken belief that functions could be segregated and the city be divided into functional zones for housing, commerce, industry, etc. The result of this however has neither strengthened the city nor created more efficient transportation systems. Most of the road systems and the capacity of public transit systems in such planning concepts must be designed for the rush-hour traffic which is usually one-directional. Only one half of the system is used under these conditions into the downtown in the morning and out of the downtown in the evening. Furthermore, for non-rush-hour times, most urban transportation systems are underused and costly to operate.

The moment, however, urban uses are interchanged, the pressure of the rush-hour can be diminished. Traffic ceases to be one-directional and therefore allows for a more efficient use of all transportation systems. But such interchange of urban uses also reduces the need for transportation for a certain percentage of the public. Kwantes (1972), in his analysis of multi-use centres, estimates aggregate savings in travel time of between 20 to 30 per cent compared with the car trips required by using monofunctional facilities.

Such reduction of transportation use, through physical adjacency, is not a contradiction to the concept that a good urban transportation system creates functional adjacency and a reinforcement of urban life. Urban multi-use reduces the cost of transportation by lessening the need for it, allowing at the same time a more efficient distribution of the ridership and finally improving the opportunity of choice.

Recreation
Definition

Recreation is defined by the Oxford Dictionary as "the action or fact of being recreated by some pleasant occupation, pastime or amusement".

Using CIAM's arbitrary but helpful division of man's activities into three sections – inhabitation, work and recreation – I have included under recreation all activities that are not part of the inhabitation function, yet are not considered work, even though in our society the boundaries are often vague.

A broad selection of buildings shelter recreational activities – shopping centres and retail stores, restaurants and food outlets, theatres and entertainment, sports facilities, educational buildings, religious buildings, etc.

As functions became more specialized through usage in these buildings, they required a more specific space to allow their full potential to unfold. However, such specialization also isolated and concentrated these activities, which often led to only part-time use of the urban district in which they were located and, eventually, to the deterioration of that district.

Yet at times the desire to isolate a function is not motivated by the wish to improve its efficiency, but can be traced back to "institutionalization". This is a kind of empire-building, wherein an activity originally part of the total life cycle segregated itself from that cycle and set up its own rules. School systems are an example of institutions that can lose contact with life and create their own empires. So can art museums that argue it is more important to preserve than to display.

Necessity of Future Flexibility

While extrapolation of past events seems to indicate that the future will lead to even greater centralisation of single functions sufficient examples exist to make us hope that a reversal of this direction is more likely to happen. There is no reason why schools or libraries for example could not be divided into smaller units and integrated into housing to bring about better land use within the fabric of our cities. The school and library in Toronto's St. Lawrence development is a good example of such a use.

31
Affleck, Desbarats, Dimakopoulos, Lebensold, Sise
Place Bonaventure, Montreal
Roof top

32
Minneapolis, Minnesota
Space consumed by cars

121

33

Integrating many different activities into one shelter does not mean that the efficiency of any particular activity need be reduced. However, careful assessment of the environmental factors common to a number of functions is required to determine the degree in which they can be integrated and possibly interchanged in the future. Who would have thought when the school building boom was raging that only twenty years later architects would find full-time jobs converting schools into other uses? The foresight to provide for interchangeable functions could have prevented this.

Our design of the McMaster Health Sciences Centre at Hamilton in 1968 was an attempt to develop a common environmental shelter capable of housing such diverse activities as residential accommodation, various hospital functions, research facilities, schools, factory activities, and animal shelters. Since future needs were unpredictable, a kind of universal space was needed to allow major functional changes to be made in the future.

The multi-use building properly designed could in a similar way respond to changes in urban-use patterns more readily than a monofunctional building can. Since it harbours different uses, it is also less subject to total obsolescence and can more easily accommodate new, more viable activities should the need arise.

Optimization of Function

There is a danger in attempting to improve a function by taking it out of an urban district and combining it with similar functions somewhere else. It is better to do so without removing the function from the context that stimulated it in the first place. The goal should not be ultimate efficiency, but rather the optimum efficiency available *within a human environment.* Perhaps the most glaring example of this danger is seen in the results created by removing shopping from its immediate neighbourhood and concentrating it in huge shopping plazas.

The thought of recreation in the urban context most frequently brings to mind the idea of highly organized centres removed from other aspects of city life. Sports fields, fitness institutes, yacht clubs – all these exist as isolated islands. And yet the best recreation offered by a city is frequently overlooked by planners. It is that impromptu recreation of walking in a park or sauntering along a downtown street, enjoying the surrounding sights, with their bustle and vitality.

In the Paris of Haussmann, this activity had been elevated into an art that fused all elements of the street together to create an entertainment full of fascination: *the theatre of the street.*

Shopping: Attempts to Optimize a Function Gone Awry
The Shopping Centre

The greatest threat to the traditional city street that once teemed with pedestrian life is the suburban shopping centre. It siphons the activator of street life, the individual store, out of the urban setting and transposes it to the isolated regional shopping centre.

We still have not adjusted to the social changes this has brought. We now question if the gain achieved in creating more efficient shopping justifies the resulting deterioration of the traditional downtown. But we must study the shopping centre's success and the rules under which it functions, for these lessons should be used in planning multi-use buildings for the downtown.

Paradoxically, the first shopping centres were a romantic recreation of the old pedestrian village street that had been lost in the suburbs. Victor Gruen was the father of this concept. Low density suburban land patterns had led to the disbursement of shopping activities into haphazard strip developments, fore-runners of the concentrated shopping centre. The concentration of these activities in shopping centres appealed to the shopper because he was presented with a visually coherent and functional market-place that contained a great variety of stores in a pleasant atmosphere. The pedestrian was not threatened in his activities by the motor car, even though surrounded by a moat of cars that confined his movements inside the centre.

Success in organizing suburban retail facilities spread with the growth of the suburbs. Later development of the shopping centre enclosed the mall and gave the village street a climatically-sealed environment which brought eternal spring into the centre. Its success further siphoned off the strength of adjacent downtown areas.

As North American housing moved from the downtown, leaving only the lowest social strata there, shopping followed it. In cities with no strongly established downtown-related transportation systems, regional shopping cent-

33
Mt. Pleasant, Toronto
School isolated from community

34
Street life in front of store

35
Victor Gruen
Eastland Shopping Centre

36
Re-creation of old pedestrian village

34

35

res came close to destroying downtown trade. The reasons were three-fold: first, accessibility by car and parking was far superior; second, the internal environment was better and pedestrian-oriented; and third, a fact often not sufficiently appreciated, taxes and building costs in outlying suburbs were less than they were downtown.

Downtown Shopping

Confronted with deteriorating downtowns, planners attempted to use the shopping centre model to resuscitate the ailing heart of the city. Unfortunately these attempts were not always successful, for this prototype was placed out of context in the downtown situation.

In the suburbs, the shopping centre was an isolated happening, an oasis surrounded by parking lots. All connection with the outside was solely by car. Indeed, in many cases parking lots were so large that one needed a car to traverse them! However, the downtown had a different fabric than the suburb – not one of isolated nodes but of continuing street spaces. Many transplanted shopping centres, such as the one in Worcester, Massachusetts, closed themselves off from the downtown in which they were located and turned their backs to the city. They had forgotten that the outside edge of the shopping complex was not the end but the beginning of a transition into the city.

An interesting "reverse" phenomenon is the present transformation of large suburban shopping centres into downtowns. Their developers have recognized the lack of other urban activities in these centres and are now trying to add these missing components. Public library branches, theatres, community meeting facilities, offices, and even housing are being added to existing shopping centre complexes. Square One in Mississauga and the Sheridan Shopping Plaza in Pickering are both adding a range of urban activities to their existing prime function of shopping.

Downtown Shopping versus Shopping Centres

Whether downtown shopping can survive in open competition with regional shopping is questionable. In some areas it has survived and flourished, like Toronto's Eaton Centre. However, this Centre works within a bustling city and a strong public transportation system oriented towards the downtown. Such conditions do not exist everywhere. Many small North American cities have no downtown-oriented transit system, therefore downtown retail outlets are at a decided disadvantage to suburban shopping centres. This is unfortunate, for though both live off the same city, the latter does little to support that city's continuing health.

Customer traffic is one of the main considerations in the location of any store. A sufficient number of people must pass a store to ensure its survival. Regional shopping centres rely on car accessibility and the free parking that only low land prices permit. Downtowns must compete with this, and can only do so if public transit exists, if parking costs can be reduced through multiple uses over a 24-hour time span, and if the downtown environment is made more appealing to shoppers.

The Shopping Mall

The regional centre has spawned the shopping mall, an enclosed pedestrian walkway that joins two or more major department stores that act as magnets drawing a flux of people past interminable smaller stores placed in between. The giant poles are 20000 to 50000 square metre stores dominating and sustaining the commercial viability of smaller 20 to 400 square metre retail outlets flanking the mall.

Attempts at transferring this pattern into an urban context create certain problems. There is a conflict between the traditional open continuous city street and the closed galleria of the mall. Many traditional examples, such as the Milan Galleria or the Passages of Paris, have demonstrated that within a well thought out pedestrian network both the open street and the enclosed gallery can exist side by side. One does not necessarily destroy the other. However, a successful solution requires a full understanding and skillful handling of the problems of both. Toronto's Eaton Centre is an example of how a major galleria can be introduced successfully into an open street network, and how both open street and galleria can reinforce each other. They do not need to be mutually exclusive.

36

Economics and Shopping

Two facts are often forgotten in the politics of land use. These are:

1. The amount of retail space used in a region is a relatively constant factor related to the number of people living in that region (unless resort areas are considered). It is estimated that approximately 16 square feet of retail sales and ancillary space could be supported by one person.
2. Shopping is a major activity supporting urban life, not only through its primary direct purchasing function but also through all the secondary functions it encourages, such as window shopping, browsing, people watching, meeting people, eating, and so on.

Shopping, unlike industry, will not grow on its own but only in relation to the existing population. Therefore, any increase in retail space in an area of stable population and market must eventually displace existing retail outlets. If, through lower municipal taxes, better transportation and lower capital costs, suburban centres can be more competitive than the downtown commercial area, then they will ultimately replace the downtown as the prime shopping area. With a lessening of such activity downtown, a city begins to die.

The problem here is not one of free enterprise versus government control. The reason why municipal taxes and land costs for suburban centres are less than for downtown centres is because regulations and conventions have been discriminatory not because of actual costs. When taxes and land costs are far lower in the suburbs than in downtown areas – through regulations of various governing bodies – then of course free enterprise will "choose" to build in the suburbs, though their choice has largely been made for them by tax manipulation. The simple, damning fact is that we have allowed the creation of a system that is sapping the strength of the downtown and is destroying the health of the city.

Multi-Use Buildings and Shopping

Multi-use buildings must embrace the retail function. Shopping, the major generator of urban life, cannot be locked away from it, but must respond to the urban space.

Not only is shopping a necessary life-support system, it is also a social event. Retailers are most successful when they understand this fact.

Retail outlets in cities can be successful in streets, in passages and in galleries as long as they all partake of a connecting pedestrian network that connects points of destination. Small passages do not work if they do not connect with the urban network, and large galleries destroy the adjacent urban streets if they do not relate some of their retail activities towards them. To have an alternate access from the street is not enough. Therefore, Eaton Centre in Toronto segregated a number of shops from the mall and faced them only towards the outside street.

Shopping should not be left in isolation, but should be integrated with other facilities and linked into the downtown network. Such networks must be understood not only as being continuous but also as being a series of events with focal areas that attract pedestrians. These nodal points are essential for the development of pedestrian traffic in between. If these nodal events are too far apart, the pedestrian traffic between them will dry up and isolate them.

It is important to understand the role of shopping not only as a functional necessity, but also as a generator of urban activities through the creation of pedestrian traffic patterns essential for the unfolding of a city. This role of shopping in the urban fabric is particularly critical, since the amount of space that can be given to this activity is fixed within a given urban situation. It is an economic factor related to the size of the population served. Therefore, shopping within a multi-use building must not only respond to the internal needs of the building – functional and economical –, but also to the needs of the urban context within which it stands.

A host of problems have been created by the thoughtless distribution of shopping in the urban fabric: regional shopping centres which caused degeneration of downtown shopping in small centres; underground or "upper level"

37
Worcester, Massachusetts
Transplanted shopping centre negates
street

38
E. H. Zeidler
Eaton Centre
Street activity

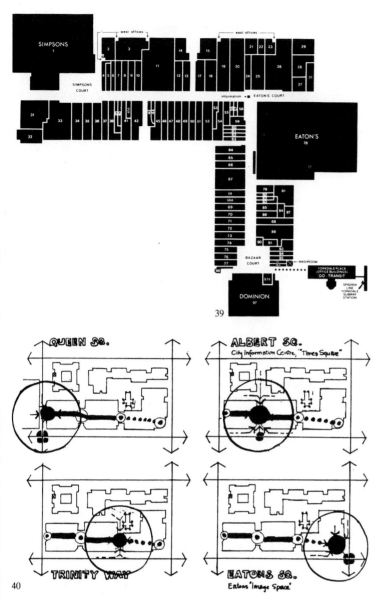

Property taxes for different municipalities within the Toronto region—1980

	Rent/sq. ft.	Property taxes/ Sq. ft.	Percentage of taxes on income of prop.
A major shopping centre in downtown Toronto	$30.	$8.00	26.7%
A major shopping centre in North York (15 miles from the centre of Toronto)	$15.00	$2.75	18.3%
A major shopping centre in Mississauga (30 miles from the centre of Toronto)	$10.00	$1.25	12.5%

pedestrian links which de-populated the streets; indiscriminate interior shopping malls which fought for a limited pedestrian traffic; shopping concentrations which atrophied the pedestrian network of a city, etc.

I do not suggest that any of the above solutions is principally right or wrong; but I do recommend that shopping areas and their distribution are one of the most important planning considerations and cannot be left to chance. Too many urban issues, beyond the profit of the individual shopkeeper, are tightly linked with it.

Other Recreational Uses

Many other recreational uses should also form part of multifunctional buildings. The principles remain the same: to correlate the different phases of urban life, to avoid segregation and isolation that would adversely affect such life, and to conserve urban space. Many recreational activities are well suited for such integration and space conservation.

Theatres

Functionally, there is no reason why a theatre should be segregated from other uses; in fact, many examples point to the opposite view. Historically the original North American cinema required a downtown location. Often, however, only the entrance was on the main street, with the main theatre on a side street connected via a gallery corridor. This gave two advantages: the street maintained its activities through stores that could front the theatre, and the bulk of the theatre could be built on cheaper land.

The Hertzberger Concert Hall in Utrecht is an ingenious example of such blending of functions. The new zoning bylaws affecting New York's Broadway are also interesting, as they encourage the inclusion of theatres into this district by using a density bonus. This bonus allows the developer to increase his permissible density if he builds a theatre in the area.

Hospitals

The Boston Hospital attempts to integrate hospital functions into the fabric of the city. Hermann Field's concept here was to move the hospital above the street level and use the street for the commercial activities that belong there. He recognized two important facts: that it is necessary to locate a hospital in the centre of city activities where the people that have to use it are, and also that a pedestrian street should not be occupied with non-pedestrian-related activities.

Unfortunately, his valid ideas remain unexecuted because they run counter to the process of "institutionalization", a process that demands isolation and clear borders for institutions. "Good fences good neighbours make!" This may be true, but it can also sap the vitality of a city.

Despite the urban need to bring pedestrian-related activities into contact with large institutions, this has always been difficult to achieve.

Parks

The urban park is one of the most versatile elements of urban recreational space. It is perhaps outside the discussion of multi-use buildings, yet multi-use buildings are affected by it as they must relate to the total urban environment.

In Canadian cities, little regard has been given to parks. The urban park is often mistakenly thought of as mere urban decoration, not as an expanded area for human activity. A small park is limited to sitting and enjoying its visual appeal. This does not diminish its importance within the urban fabric. London has used this device effectively to enhance what would have been otherwise a monotonous environment. However, a better urban pattern is achieved by a linkage of parks. This creates linear walkways that fulfill many more recreational needs than the isolated small park. Such park links need not be very wide. The Hayan Park in Kyoto creates a totally natural feeling within the narrow space of forty feet wedged into a dense urban environment. Even small snippets

39
Yorkdale, Toronto
Plan of typical shopping centre

40
E. H. Zeidler
Eaton Centre
Diagram, showing pattern of streets
and entrances

41
Toronto, Yorkdale, Mississauga
Diagram—taxes

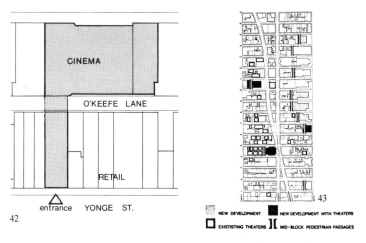

42
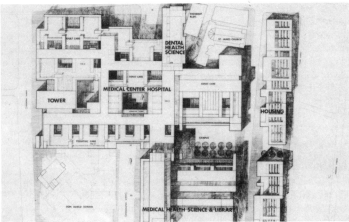

43

NEW DEVELOPMENT ☐ NEW DEVELOPMENT WITH THEATERS
☐ EXISTISTING THEATERS ☐ MID-BLOCK PEDESTRIAN PASSAGES

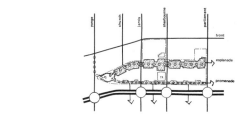

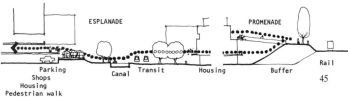

Parking
Shops
Housing
Pedestrian walk

46

of vacant city land, if imaginatively transformed into linked parks, can revitalize the often dull, grey, urban surroundings. Ontario Place is a different example of the urban park's potential to revive urban areas, in this case, Toronto's long-neglected waterfront.

The introduction of such urban parks, either in a romantic or classic form, will give the multi-use building a dimension that enriches its being. The esplanades at Pickering and St. Lawrence are examples of the classic form; Toronto's Harbour City and the Rosedale Ravine show the potential of the romantic form of urban parks. Both give the pedestrian an alternate network that adds to the city's richness and enjoyability.

Summary

It is not enough to prove the technical and functional feasibility of incorporating recreational use with other uses into a multi-use building. A new attitude is needed that encourages or better legislates such solutions if we are to ensure the survival of our downtowns and achieve a new vitality in our cities.

Market forces tend to explode and segregate the environment under the pretext of progress and greater efficiency. I have illustrated that such segregation leads to the destruction of the urban environment. Solutions can be found through the use of the multi-use building, which offers planners a building block capable of maintaining a heterogeneous and vital urban fabric.

In fact, it is particularly the multi-use building which can use urban space more effectively because of its ability to create vertical adjacencies of different activities at varying scales.

Work

The industrial city of the 19th Century attempted to segregate working and living in the hope of improving city life. Coal-fired factories with their dirt, grime and noise did not integrate well with housing. Since then, however, industry has undergone tremendous changes. Though the dream of totally-automated factories has not become the reality that was predicted, automation has nevertheless reduced the number of people working in primary industry.

Most work spaces today are not related to smoke-belching factories and can be readily integrated into any part of a city without detrimental effects. Today there is no reason why all factories must be separated from other activities of living.

Small Industry

Modern planning banished industrial plants into industrial districts, away from other living functions. While solving some problems of noise and air pollution, this often created new problems, particularly if these industries moved outside the old municipal boundary. Many times the new location was not serviced by public transit, creating difficulties for their labour force. The municipalities that harboured the old factories also suffered from such moves by having their tax base reduced.

Small, diversified workshops or factories in the downtown maintain the vitality of this urban area. It is the diversity of many interrelated activities that keeps a city alive. In fact, the smaller the average enterprise of a city, the healthier is the economic life of the city in the long run. The Region of Toronto with nearly three million people has no large, single industry with more than

42
Plan of Imperial G downtown shows theatre on Victoria and entrance on Yonge Street only

43
Broadway, New York
Incentive zoning encourages the new construction of theatres

44
The Architects' Collaborative
Tufts New England Medical Center
Integration of hospital with city fabric

45
St. Lawrence, Toronto
Esplanade
Linear walkway

46
Ontario Place, Toronto
Revival of waterfront

47

48

5000 workers. In fact, the City of Toronto has an average employment of approximately 30 people. Economic crises are much easier survived by such a city than by a single base manufacturing town, such as Detroit, for example.

The employment that small workshops can provide for a wide sector of the downtown population is vitally important for the economic life of a city.

As the efficiency of suburban shopping centres siphoned small stores out of the downtown, so did suburban industrial parks draw the small workshop from the downtown area. Offices that could afford to pay higher rents replaced this type of small enterprise but not necessarily to the advantage of the city.

The Economics of Small Industry surviving in Cities

It is not just a romantic longing for diversity but a necessity for cities to encourage and provide space for small industry and workshops within their downtown areas. But even if such industrial use is permitted in an urban core region, it will not take hold there unless affordable space is available. Unfortunately, like a nearly-extinct species, small industry at present can only live under the cover of protection. Small workshops or industries must take into consideration many economic factors.

The main ones are: cost of land rental; cost of building rental; cost of taxes; closeness to markets; and availability of a work force.

Unskilled labour may be found more easily on the fringes of the downtown area than in the suburbs which usually lack intensive public transportation. The presence of this unskilled work force may be enough encouragement to keep industry downtown, notwithstanding the higher costs of remaining there.

Zoning regulations must play a protective role and take into consideration the fact that small industry can only afford low land rents. Presently, the Toronto City Council is attempting to keep industry in its downtown, despite the lure of cheaper, better accommodation in the suburbs for industry, and the pressures of downtown office and housing expansion. The hope is to limit these more profitable land uses through zoning restrictions so they won't totally displace existing industrial uses.

Including industrial work space within multi-use buildings, while desirable for the life of the city, is a problem beyond the control of the individual building; it is a problem that only the municipalities can control and solve if they wish to maintain their economic base of work places.

To achieve a healthy urban environment, cheap space must be available for uses that otherwise could not exist in such high-cost surroundings. Artists and artisans' workshops, places for the small entrepreneur to start an out-of-the ordinary business, room for the school teacher whose hobby is repairing Jaguars, space for the man who wants to build a boat, refinish old cars or upholster furniture and so on – such variety vitalizes urban life and complements it. The physical surroundings for these enterprises are often secondary, as these workshops grow on the enthusiasm and overtime work of their owners. Their attention is wrapped up in what they are doing, rather than in their surroundings. Such affordable space must be available for them in the city. Jane Jacobs has pointed out that one of the most vital functions of a city is the incubation of new industries. This requires the availability of cheap space. In Toronto, successful enterprises got their start in residential garages and if you walk the back alleys of Toronto you can see the evidence of this illegal activity.

The Multi-Use Building as a Habitat for Small Industry

Many small industries can adjust their physical requirements to fit into left-over loft spaces. We can also easily use otherwise wasted interior space in a multi-use building which is particulary suited to include such activities as small industry can utilize spaces that are not very well suited for other functions.

The integration of such industrial uses with other functions makes good sense in situations where greater densities are essential. Dimitri Procos in "Mixed Land Use", however, points out that the use of elevators in multi-level factories creates four times higher operational costs than one-level-loading factories have. Therefore, to achieve efficiency and density, we must design multi-use buildings to house industry on the loading level only, and use the other levels for different activities.

Space could even be created underneath urban parks for small industry to use. This was successfully done in downtown Helsinki where an urban park sits above an industrial plant.

47
Ontario Place, Toronto

48
Haydan Park, Kyoto
Example of narrow urban park

Industrial space, however, must be designed to permit readily changes in size and function. Experience has shown that the organization of most industrial processes change many times during the life span of the building which houses them. The space must be able to accommodate these changes.

Office Space
Office Towers: The Present Prototype of Office Space

As shopping centres were the dominant building form to consider in our discussion on recreation, so must the office tower be considered as the dominant form in any discussion of office space. Before one can suggest alternate solutions it is important to understand why the office tower became the prototype for office buildings, particularly in North America. Here technology developed the elevator and the high-rise steel frame construction technique. The ability to build more densely in conjunction with uncontrolled land speculation created the office tower, modern architecture simplified it into its notorious box-like form. These towers were called by many the tombstone of the city and with their wind-swept plazas they seemed to become the killer of city life. Yet even though the office tower has also been decried as being degrading to the human worker and his needs, it has prevailed in our cities.

Despite totally different building regulations, this building type emerged in New York, Houston, London, Paris – in fact, everywhere. Office towers have been built both in cities where zoning bylaws encourage them, and in cities where laws attempted to prevent their creation. The reasons for the dominance of this type are many:

Adaptability of Office Space

As businesses and organizations change with time, so do their demands change as to the space they need. For a building to survive such changes, it must have adaptable space. This flexibility of space must be designed into the building, it does not happen by accident.

Building owners who rent office space to others require even more flexible space than do owners that occupy their own office space. In order to rent successfully (and thus be able to carry the maintenance and mortgage costs), they must have space that appeals to many different clients. Without such flexible space the owner will either be forced into bankruptcy due to the marginal nature of building financing, or will be forced to replace the building with one that will return the necessary income.

Optimum Floor Areas and Tenant Size

The preferred office building has a minimum net rentable area of 1500 to 2000 square metres per floor.

Smaller floor areas are not attractive to tenants requiring large areas, for they would then need too many floors to accommodate their organization. Nor would floor areas much larger than 2000 square metres be attractive to small tenants, for they would lose their identity. Long corridors past innumerable doors belonging to other organizations would not give the tenant the sense of identity that he is looking for.

Another advantage of this size is that horizontal relationships for large organizations seem to reach a satisfactory efficiency, and vertical separation into various floors – though less effective than horizontal adjacency – becomes acceptable.

Most office buildings have a mixture of tenant sizes. We found that particularly the most prestigious downtown offices reveal a rent roll with many tenants using very small spaces. The necessity of accommodating both small and large tentants determines the optimum size of the office floor.

Garage Service Workshop Court Studio Café Plaza

Dwellings Court Brigantine Delivery Assembly

49

50

49
Harbour City
Workshop space integrated

50
Factory in Helsinki

51
TD Centre
Office prototype, for optimum floor layout

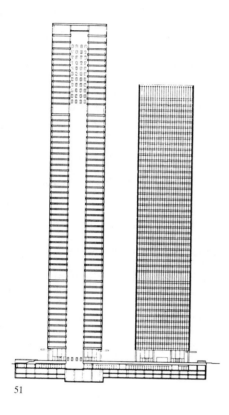

51

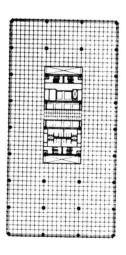
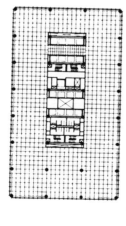

The Centre Core Office Tower

The free-standing tower has become standardized and dominates today's downtown.

The efficiency of its floor layout, while dependent on different building codes, works basically on the principle that all vertical functions – elevators and mechanical devices, washrooms, fire exits, etc. – are placed in the centre of the floor, allowing open loft-type office space to surround this core.

A well-designed office floor should achieve 90 to 95% rentable floor space and should have a depth of not more than 10 to 14 metres from core to window wall. This allows reasonable light penetration to the core, enables subdivision of the floor into smaller tenancies, and permits relatively short corridors in cases of multiple tenancy.

Problems of the Centre Core Layout

However, such optimum floor size limits the number of work stations that can have immediate adjacency to a window. I think that there cannot be any doubt that the majority of office tasks are performed better in an environment that has natural daylight, rather than in an artificially-lit one.

To observe the changes of natural daylight, to create a sense of time and place, to have the ability to change focus to far-away views are important elements to consider. Of course the average distance of the work station to a window could be shortened by convoluting the exterior surfaces in a central core office plan or by stretching the central core. However, both reduce the floor-space efficiency and in turn increase construction and operating costs.

Working Environment

Working conditions for office employees have undergone many changes in the last decades. The satisfaction derived is not only related to the type of work, the fellow-workers and management, but also to the physical working environment. This not only includes the individual work space and the atmosphere of the total office space, it is also affected by the way the office relates inside and outside of the building to other activities including transportation.

An office that is removed from restaurants and other city facilities will have to provide its own cafeteria or lunch room, and sometimes also recreational facilities for games or reading. Such places, however, may be shunned by workers if different ones are provided nearby outside the office.

Individual preferences will emphasize varying aspects of the office environment as being important. The type of working place to be preferred will depend on the type of employees, the type of work done, and the business's social status. It is impossible to establish formal, fixed rules for the environmental requirements of an office.

However, there are some requirements that are universal: daylight and a view are usually preferred if they can be provided; the absence of noise and a sense of privacy without isolation is another requirement; the freedom to do, within reason, your own thing in your own space without being bothered by or bothering others is important. Some people enjoy absolute neatness and apparently cannot function without it, whereas others work well within a creative "mess": both types are often annoyed and bothered by people who do the opposite. Therefore to have the ability to allow for these needs is important.

Another environmental asset is the adaptability of office space discussed earlier. Work patterns in offices shift and the space must adjust to it. Building forms that are tailored to only one function often have problems adjusting to new ones. The most advantageous spaces are those close to both people circulation and daylight. Such spaces can be most easily adapted to later changes.

Land Cost and Building Height

The height of an office building is related to land cost. Despite advances in technology, the costs of the building structure and mechanical systems increase exponentially as the building rises. The efficiency of the building diminishes due to the increased space demands for mechanical and elevator systems.

The increased cost of constructing higher buildings must be balanced against the reduced land cost through greater density, and higher rents obtainable due to the prestige of occupying a tall building. While in the individual situation those calculations may make financial sense, one must relate these calculations to the city as a whole and the land use within the city. It is incongruous and economically absurd to erect a 110-storey building in the midst of under-used urban land (Sears Tower in Chicago), if one looks at it from the economic framework of a city.

129

52

53

Integration of Office Towers within the Downtown

If we accept the necessity of the office tower we must carefully integrate these huge structures into the urban context and thoughtfully create a relation between them and other urban activities.

Such integration into the North American downtown has often been based strictly on financial land cost considerations. Little has been done to explore a more meaningful integration into the urban context.

The pedestrian environment created at ground level by most huge office buildings is unpleasant. It is at this level where the modern office tower interferes most with the downtown activity. Creating such monoliths isolated in their own plazas may be good for the corporate spirit, but does little for the city. In fact, where such usage has become predominant, it has damaged the life of the street.

Many seemingly contradictory issues must be resolved at the ground level. The office tower needs its own prestigious entrance but it also must be part of the street activity at this level. It must be related to people. Wind and sun penetration must be carefully considered to avoid a detrimental influence on the pedestrian environment.

A sense of identity is essential for the office tenants, who demand a prestigious entrance. Yet it is possible for the office lobby to give such a sense of identity and still be related to the more mundane but livelier activities of the street such as shopping and restaurants. Toronto's Dundas Street Tower is an example of such integration, without losing identity.

Planning Advantages of Using Office Blocks

An analogy might be drawn between the office tower and the Parisian walk-up blocks of Haussmann that were suitable for a wide spectrum of needs, such as apartments, offices or shops. The planner could use them without determining their end use in his initial urban planning concept.

The form of a city could be determined with these blocks that were capable of taking on various functions at a later time. They could also, over a period of time, adjust their functions to new needs without destroying the unity of the urban space created.

The well-planned modern office building could give a similar potential. It can be built without particular tenants in mind. With a few exceptions, it will fulfill many of the needs a tenant may have – prestigious location, impressive entrance, short distance from elevator to individual office, freedom of layout, built-in environmental controls, maximum window space, good horizontal communications, easy separation between tenants, and security for each individual tenant. Though these requirements can probably be achieved in other building forms, few at the moment have achieved them as economically as the office tower has.

The Atrium-Type Office Building

Of course, there are alternates to the centre core plan, but they have been little explored at present. One of the most promising new forms is the atrium building. Through its configuration it is able to provide many elements demanded by the office user better than the centre core tower. For example, it can provide a greater floor area with better proximity of working place to window. Because of this, fewer floors are needed to accommodate the same number of workers, a saving in operating and building costs. The closed interior court reduces energy loss. By putting the elevators into the atrium they can be transformed into an existing circulation and orientation system.

The Multi-Use Building and the Office

Flexibility of use is a major urban need. Despite the arguments that the single-use, conventional office building at present appears to be the most efficient solution, it stands to reason that if the flexibility of the office building can also accommodate other uses, the life expectancy of such a building should be greater. Perhaps the conversion of many older downtown New York office towers into apartments may support my statement. In addition, the mixture of different activities creates a much more enjoyable ambience for people using the building.

52
Sears Tower

53
TD Centre
Monolithic tower, windswept plaza

54
E. H. Zeidler
Eaton Centre, Dundas Tower
Diagram. Lobby relating to other functions

55
Le Corbusier
La Ville Radieuse
Loss of street

130

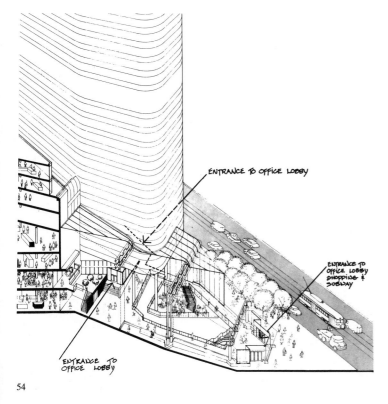

ENTRANCE TO OFFICE LOBBY

ENTRANCE TO OFFICE LOBBY SHOPPING & SUBWAY

ENTRANCE TO OFFICE LOBBY

54

55

External Forces

Architecture is in a period of re-evaluation. An era has come to its end and we are looking at what it has meant to us.

Prevailing architectural theories have overlooked the fact that no building within an urban situation stands alone. We forgot that a building is a link in the urban chain, and as such must respond to urban needs as much as to its own. The demand for structural and functional honesty that modern architecture called for resulted in a rather selfish individuality that didn't always integrate with its surroundings. The modern city was thought of largely as a "visual happening", and this encouraged such individual performance.

Le Corbusier's Ville Radieuse was a radically new concept of the city of tomorrow. In his designs, the street – one of the main images of the city past – was eliminated as a three-dimensional space and became a two-dimensional function spatially unrelated to the buildings which created it. Buildings were transformed into isolated, self-contained *objets d'art*. This prototype of a modern city was clung to with surprising tenacity, for over half a century, considering that these planning principles resulted in so many failures.

The apparent mistakes of such planning were brushed away as birth pains or shortcomings in execution of a basically sound idea. Only when a total re-evaluation of modern architecture's theories began was the flaw in their concepts exposed. But this discovery did not come quickly. It evolved from many individual questions that slowly set up an overwhelming evidence that modern planning ideas were based on misguided attitudes towards the city.

One of the first questioners of these modern concepts was Jane Jacobs. With the unobstructed vision of a non-planner she queried why these lofty ideals did not achieve what they promised to do. In fact, she pointed out that the lowly older sections of Greenwich Village slated for urban renewal and demolition worked much better. Was this a paradox? Were we missing an essential issue in our understanding of urban life? With her inquiry a shift in our attitude towards modern architecture and planning began that today is changing our environment.

The external demands that act on the urban environment have an equal if not stronger influence on the individual building than its internal demands. Modern architectural philosophy was not willing to accept a compromise between external and internal demands, yet it is precisely the acceptance of this compromise that shapes individual buildings within the urban context. If such an attitude of compromise is rejected, the individual building will irreconcilably clash with its urban environment to the detriment of both. Our cities are filled with examples of such conflict, where a building's design, in not adapting internal functions to the requirements of the urban situation, has damaged the urban environment.

For a building to merely be in the urban context is not enough; it must also participate. Unfortunately, few modern buildings, particulary in North America, participate in city life. Most of them have only tended to their own problems. Many examples of multi-use buildings shown in Part II of this book still lack such integration within the urban situation.

It is difficult in some situations to rebuild an urban fabric after it has been lost. Many of the North American examples used in Part II were an attempt to rectify a deteriorated urban area. It is obvious that such projects cannot physically go beyond their boundaries, yet the gesture they embody towards their surroundings is important. It will not only influence what happens at the edges of the project but also beyond into the city. However, if such gesture becomes a dividing wall, then the project's connection with the city may be broken forever. The Renaissance Centre in Detroit, despite its lively inner activities, remains a beautiful architectural statement that separates itself from its urban neighbourhood. The Eaton Centre, in contrast, tries to blend its edges and respond to its urban surroundings.

In the following pages I will look at external needs that influence the shape of individual buildings within the urban context. Three different though tightly interrelated viewpoints are involved. First I will talk about *urban space,* what it means, and how it works as a static three-dimensional, mainly visual element within the city. Then I will discuss *urban movement patterns,* how they are created, what they do, and their integrity within the urban environment. And lastly, I will examine the *urban political structure* within which cities are built and which their forms ultimately express.

131

Atrium Office Building

The basic inefficiency inherent in the centre-core, conventional office-tower solution is its narrow cross-section (limited inside by the psychologically maximum distance from the core to the window). This affects all the four major components of the building: the structure, the elevators, the curtain wall and the mechanical.

By introducing an atrium, the following is achieved: the floor area is increased, and at the same time the distance to the window is shortened; the building height is lowered, which allows the use of an inexpensive flat-slab concrete structure rather than a more sophisticated steel structure. This also reduces the number of elevators, their shaft length and the number of stops. In addition, the exterior envelope is condensed and the cost of the mechanical system, which is a function of the exterior skin, is decreased.

56a
Sectional view

56b
Front view

56c
Typical floor plan

56d
Cost comparison

56e
Relationship to the city

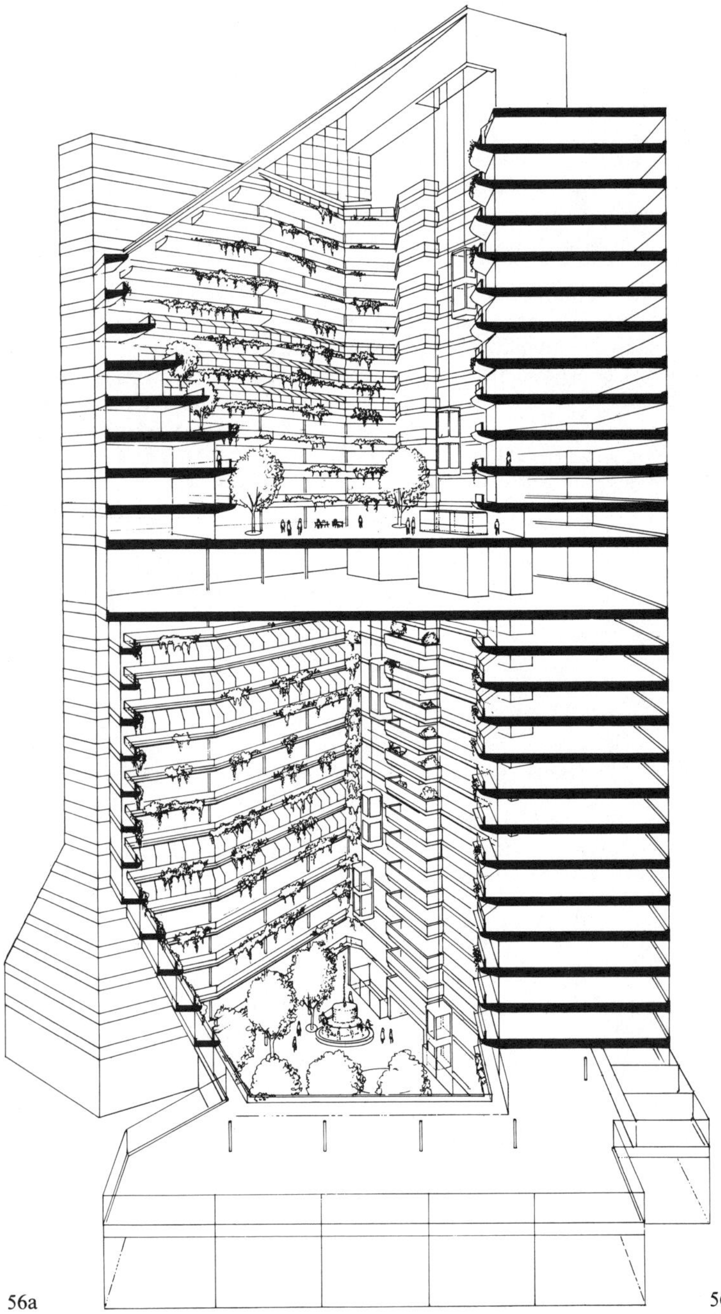

56a

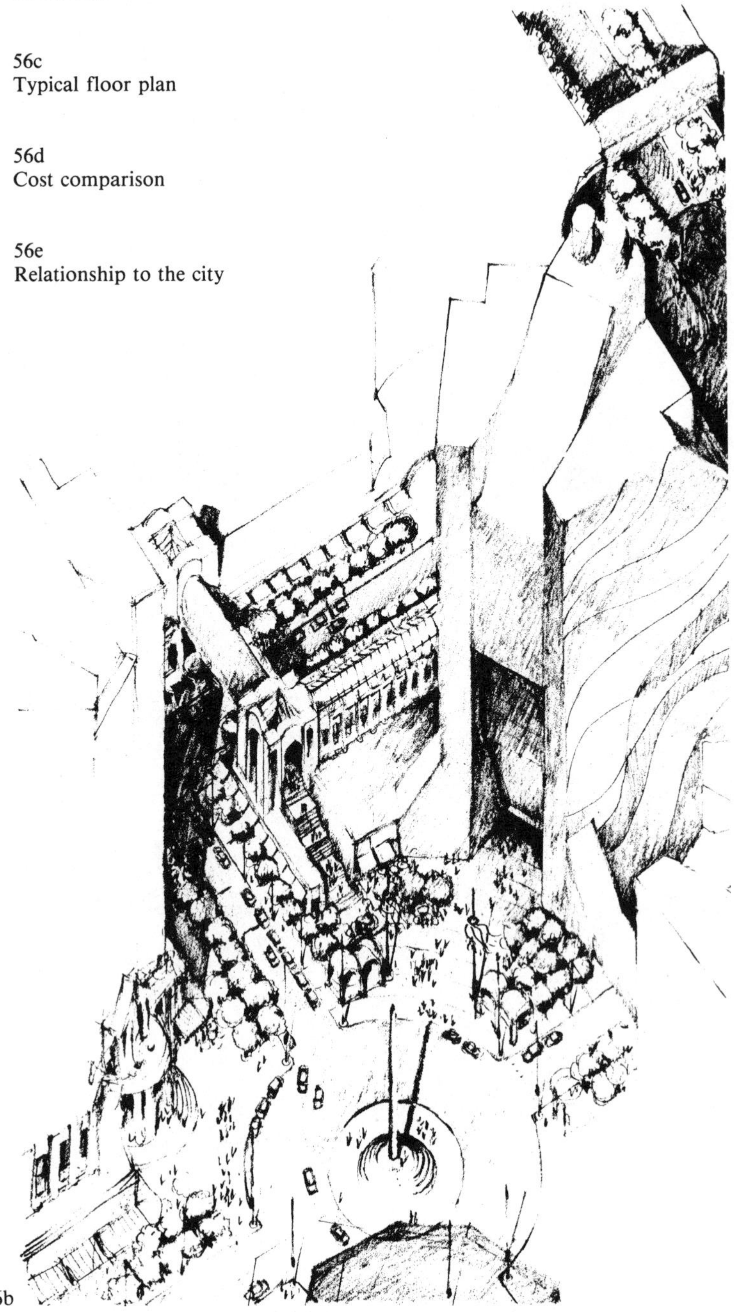

56b

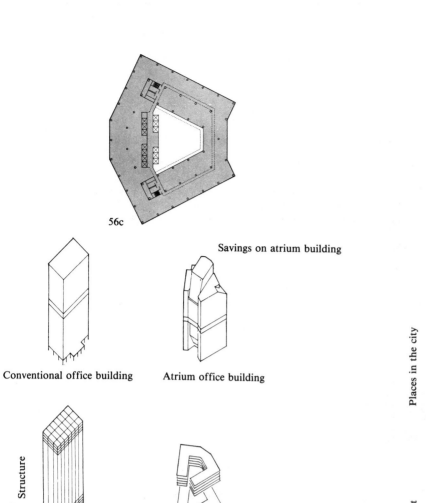

56c

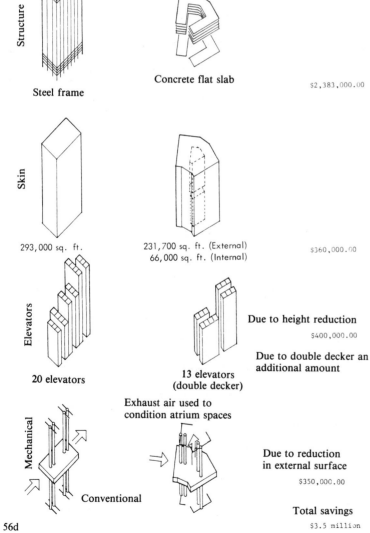

Conventional office building

Atrium office building

Savings on atrium building

Structure

Steel frame

Concrete flat slab

$2,383,000.00

Skin

293,000 sq. ft.

231,700 sq. ft. (External)
66,000 sq. ft. (Internal)

$360,000.00

Elevators

20 elevators

13 elevators
(double decker)

Due to height reduction
$400,000.00

Due to double decker an
additional amount

Mechanical

Conventional

Exhaust air used to
condition atrium spaces

Due to reduction
in external surface
$350,000.00

Total savings
$3.5 million

56d

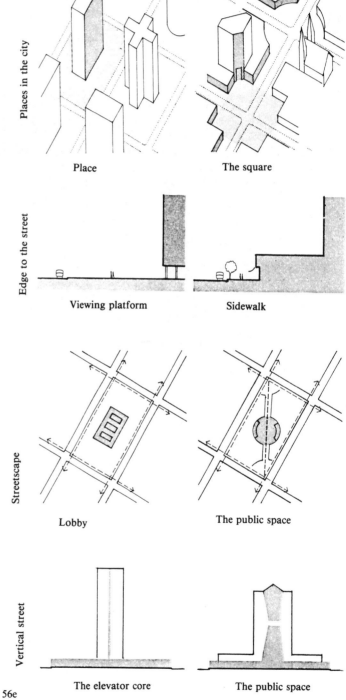

Places in the city

Conventional

Place

The square

Edge to the street

Viewing platform

Sidewalk

Streetscape

Lobby

The public space

Vertical street

The elevator core

The public space

56e

133

57

58

Urban Space

Our cities are becoming large urban conglomerations. The choice to abandon them is only open to a few. The question for most is not of where to live, but of how to live in them. Our task is to deal with these Goliaths, to prevent them from suppressing us and to make the city environment again enjoyable to live in.

We must begin by understanding our urban environment. But how do we understand a city? It is not through individual buildings or monuments, no matter how important they are by themselves. Other than acting as identifiers, monuments do not form the city we live in. We understand our cities through their urban spaces: their streets and plazas – literally the negative of what we call architecture. The summation of individual building façades form the enclosures of these urban spaces, the *Stadtraum*.

Internal versus External Needs

It has been said that Western architecture only escaped from the sculptural monument of the Egyptian pyramids into true architecture when it developed the inside space. We can extend this statement to urban architecture which only came into existence when it began to use individual architecture as sub-elements of a greater, urban unity.

When architecture acknowledges being part of a greater urban whole, then external demands have equal or more influence on an individual building than its internal needs. Further reflection will make it apparent that even the internal needs of each building result from its urban existence. Therefore, individual buildings must accept the existence of a higher urban order, and subordinate themselves to it. The denial of such a superior order within the urban fabric has deeply damaged our cities, particularly in North America. When structures are built only with regard to their internal needs, disregarding their responsibility to external urban demands, then no coherent urban unity can exist.

The current, widely accepted denial of such an urban order can be traced back to many assumed axioms that formed part of modern architectural philosophy: that the individuality of a building is supreme; that the street as urban space is inconsequential; and so on.

The City Street

The thing most necessary to make lively cities is to revive the street. Wherever the modern city street has been compared with the old city street, the latter usually won hands down. This was not only because we have an emotional attachment to the history of our old cities, but also because the old city and its street provided a way of life that we miss today.

Human beings are, by and large, sociable and gregarious creatures. They love to be with others, enjoy to see and be seen, to talk and listen – and one of the nicer places to do those things is on a lively city street. Ultimately, all activities in life are social functions, even working. An environment that does not promote social intercourse will eventually not be used by people.

Shopping as a merely functional activity will not be as successful and acceptable as shopping that is treated as a social activity. The traditional shopping street fulfilled these additional social functions exceedingly well. It provided many diversions, easy accessibility, and a visual coherence that created a space attractive to be in. It combined shopping with other activities, multiplied urban life, and furthermore made the environment safe. In this context the street is more than the mere functional connector to which Urban Planners had relegated it. In its ultimate fulfillment as a social space the street becomes the theatre in which actors and audience interchange their roles.

The street as "theatre" is a powerful social draw. Paris illustrates this best. Parisian sidewalk cafés unabashedly set their chairs side by side, not to look at each other but to look at the street as though watching a play. And despite our motorization, it is still only as a pedestrian that a human being can partake of such social contact.

In reality, the street's form and the activities it generates are one, as in a good play both stage-setting and action complement each other. However, I wish to talk here about static stage-setting and its significance in the overall play. I hope to prove that in urban planning stage-setting is as important as stage-action, and if we neglect the first, even the best urban play will suffer.

59

The Urban Framework

Many city planners are now trying to bring all the necessary components back into the street life. To help accomplish this, we architects must again accept that individual buildings play a supporting role within the urban context, in fact, that they can only exist within that framework. Without accepting an urban fabric, without working with it and making our designs complement it, we will not be able to build and maintain the cities we are longing for.

We cannot reproduce the traditional street by simply conjuring up images of the Victorian city and reproducing them with modern façades – *à la* Krier – without allowing for the functions that they should contain to unfold properly. Content and urban form both are needed to create the tapestry of city life; only by accepting the duality of these two existences will we again give vitality to our cities.

The activity of the street and public square in their manifold variations are inseparably connected with the visual form of the individual buildings which physically support this activity. Form and activity cannot live without each other. Their interaction does not result in a uniform pattern but in a multi-faceted variety. Visually, such an urban contexture would be linked more to the Collage City promulgated by Colin Rowe than to the formal monotony demanded by modern city design.

Such collage cities do not require the grand unity of Baroque design, yet do need a continuum of space joining their diverse parts, space that is based on urban need and a sense of historicism. However, this urban collage should not emanate the aura of a collector's item prevalent in Colin Rowe's model. Each part of such an urban contexture should have a diversity that relates to itself. For example, a street is given a comprehensive and active form through its many diverse buildings, yet all the buildings should acknowledge the street as the ordering form, – a continuation of concept that relates to the greater order of the city and melts together the different parts of such urban contextures.

The multi-use building must accept such urban framework as the guiding force that controls its form; the organization of its internal uses must respond to these urban needs. We cannot plan such buildings only from within as an expression of functions and financial needs, but must conceive it also within the external urban fabric. Of course, that presumes the existence of urban design principles for a particular district. Ideally this could be evolved as each building is designed, if the designer for each building has the economic power to accept the limitation of these urban principles. For example, if needed to complete with his building a façade at a given height, rather than build an isolated tower that may be less costly to build.

Unfortunately, in reality there is little hope to create a coherent urban space in an urban situation where many owners control the land, unless some of the urban space principles are predetermined and become part of the land control. A situation that presently does not exist as a general rule in North America.

The Façade: More than an Expression of Function

Once we accept the guiding order of a greater urban framework, then many attitudes towards architectural design will change. One of these is our attitude towards the façade. An influential theory of modern architecture was that a building had to be a truthful expression of its inner needs. For this reason, the façade had to reflect these needs in its external form, and had to express this inner "truth" equally on all sides. In other words, the building became a magnified sculpture, an *objet d'art* that obviously took consideration of its environment, yet still remained centred within itself.

Urban buildings constructed before this modern theory came into vogue dealt with their façades quite differently. Camillo Sitte, a nineteenth-century Viennese urban planner, studied the churches of Rome and showed that out of two hundred and fourteen, only six churches were free-standing. All the others were built-in and related to the various urban spaces they faced, the front perhaps to a square, the back to a small street. Each façade responded to its particular environment and not only was each side often different from the other, but neither did they necessarily reflect the building's inner "truth".

The Chapel of Hildebrandt in Balthasar Neumann's Palais at Würzburg is an exciting example of such difference in expression. In fact, both inside and outside play totally different roles. The façade complements the civic function of the square it faces and is part of this composition; the chapel interior fulfills a different emotional function that addresses itself only to the worshipper after he has entered. The nearly overwhelming spiritual atmosphere that engulfs him would have been dissipated had it also been expressed in the façade. It is the tension between the exterior and interior that creates this powerful experience.

57
J. Portman
Renaissance Center, Detroit
Broken connection between project and city

58
E. H. Zeidler
Eaton Centre, Yonge Street
Blending of edges in response to urban surroundings

59
Champs Elysées, Paris
Sidewalk café as stage set for the theatre of the street

60

61

The façade, belittled and smiled upon by modern architects, is a serious element within urban design. In simile, it is the face with which we greet our friends. We express with a smile their always welcome presence – even if we sometimes wish they had not dropped in at that very moment.

Urban architecture has a broader role than merely expressing a building's functions. The concept that architecture is the exposure of internal function in the exterior façade can lead to confusion in the urban context. During a building's life cycle, many functions may in turn be housed within the same shell; however, it is the façade of that shell which forms the lasting urban space. We must recognize that the meaning of the façade must reflect and is related to its urban context.

In Summary

Since this treatise is not on urban design, but rather on the multifunctional building, I have tried to cover only those points in which the multi-use building has to accept influences from the urban fabric. I have therefore not discussed the possibilities and options such a framework has in itself.

I would like to state here that I do not envisage such a framework to be limited to the vocabulary of a Haussmann's Paris, incapable of accepting the high-rise, incapable of accepting open planning, incapable of accepting other elements advocated by modern planners. These new elements cannot be brushed away. Though they are not all-powerful, they are nevertheless viable and must be considered in forming the city.

The multi-use building is an idea, a concept, not a definite form. It can be used as a building block to help create a vibrant urban space. As such, the multi-use concept must embrace and respond to all elements that modern urban life demands, not only the functional needs of today but also the emotional needs that have been shaped by our past heritage.

Multi-use buildings are part of the urban stage-setting that creates the visual container of urban life. As there are literary persons who do not see the unity between stage-setting and action, the *Gesamtkunstwerk,* but only conceive the word as all important, so are there city planners who concentrate on the urban action only and miss the visual setting as a vital part of the whole. We have lost the art of urban design that concerns itself with this visual setting. The reasons are manifold; the misguided principles of modern architecture are only part of them. But understanding their failure, accepting the individual building as subordinate to a greater urban order, can help us again to create the political and legal atmosphere necessary for a visually integrated, coherent urban environment.

Urban Movement Patterns

Cities live or die as their ability to communicate waxes or wanes. Communication in the urban context means movement. It is the hustle, crowding and apparent confusion of the metropolis that makes them so exciting and alive. Yet to many modern planners, this confusion is something that has to be reduced if not eliminated.

The arrival of the motor car magnified the urban traffic problems, yet vehicular traffic was already a problem in ancient Rome. Caesar attempted to resolve it by restricting the times during which vehicles could move. Leonardo da Vinci suggested vertical segregation of vehicular and pedestrian traffic. The introduction of traffic segregation was also propagated by Le Corbusier. It is, in principle, a sound concept as long as it is not canonized and held to be the only way to resolve urban traffic.

To a certain degree an apparent traffic confusion is necessary in urban life. Manhattan is vibrant, not despite but because it is nearly impossible to move

60
Balthasar Neumann
Bishop's Palais
Exterior as response to civic function

62
Le Corbusier
Drawing. Traffic segregation

61
Lukas von Hildebrandt
Schlosskapelle, Würzburg
Interior. Baroque spiritual exhuberance

136

62

about in a car. Such traffic confusion has a hidden discipline which sets its own equilibrium. Too much tampering with this apparent confusion can endanger a city's vitality. For example, expressways introduced into metropolitan areas to speed traffic flow and relieve the congestion of city streets often harm the urban fabric more than they help resolve traffic problems. They destroy the neighbourhoods through which they are carved and force more cars into the downtown than its space can stand, thereby inflicting on the downtown all problems connected with cars: increased traffic congestion, increased parking space, increased pollution and noise, decreased pedestrian movement, and deterioration of commercial space. Lastly, the expressway prevents the active development of a transit system.

The downtown area cannot be served by cars alone. Urban density requires public transit as its predominant transportation mode. Only then can the pedestrian movement be achieved that maintains the life of the downtown.

But far from recognizing the threat that the car represented to the downtown, modern planners at the beginning of this century saw the car as the great liberator of our future urban life. Frank Lloyd Wright hoped that his Broad-Acres would eventually supplant the need to live in cities. Each American could root in eternal bliss on his own acre of land, liberated from the city by the car. Le Corbusier's plans maintained the density of the city, but he also felt that the structure of the city could be reorganized with the help of the car and modern technology to create an image of a natural park in the city.

Planning Theories based on Le Corbusier's Models
The most significant visual models for city planners in the last decades have been concepts developed by Le Corbusier. Not only did he suggest segregating and ordering the main functions of urban life into different parts of the city, but he also planned to untangle the confusion of traffic by isolating and segregating its different modes. The car, as man's symbol of future freedom, played a major role in Le Corbusier's cities; unfortunately, its menacing reality was not foreseen at that time of euphoria.

Streets were segregated according to the various modes of traffic – pedestrian, vehicular, etc. – and also according to the speeds of motor vehicles using them – collector, throughway, etc. The traditional street as a three-dimensional urban space was deliberately abolished by Le Corbusier. He once actually apologized and corrected a plan that had the vestige of a three-dimensional street in it. To him the street represented all the squalor that cities of the past contained. An amazing viewpoint to be held by an architect who lived in Paris!

The modern city street, under Le Corbusier's guiding hand, became a two-dimensional ribbon of transportation that merely joined points of destination. Le Corbusier suggested lifting vehicular streets into the air so that pedestrians would have the ground to themselves and would never meet with a car.

The building's interior became the arrival point, not the city street outside. Buildings themselves were set on pilotis so people not only walked past but also underneath the buildings without noticing them or the activities they contained but to allow the Park on the Groundplan to flow uninterrupted. The pedestrian, when not within the building, was relegated to pleasant walks through this park. Footpaths did not run parallel to the streets but criss-crossed to create the shortest connections between two buildings. The street as an urban place "to be" had disappeared, and with it went its urban life. The people that Le Corbusier envisaged to live in his cities were, when not working, supposed to act as if on a holiday, sunning on roof tops, walking in isolated green parks, doing in every aspect the opposite of what they would do in the reality of the Parisian street. In a strange way they were perhaps related to Hemingway's heroes that existed outside the ordinary life.

The life style that Le Corbusier envisaged was anti-urban. It was an attempt to transform the city into a rural resort. Such a concept is understandable as an attempt to escape from the industrial city. However the failure to understand the complexity of the urban matrix did great damage to our cities, especially in the planning of new towns and suburbs where this concept became gospel. The tragic thing about many of these theories is that they are not outrightly wrong, but that they do not have the universal applicability that their creators proclaimed for them.

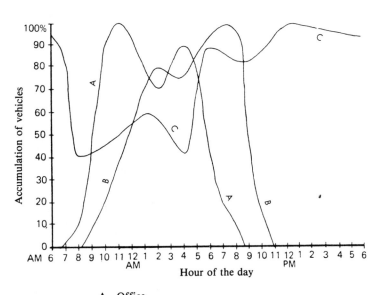

A Office
B Retail
C Residential

63

Public Transportation

A modern city cannot exist without public transportation. It vitally affects a city's present and future growth. However, a city does not exist for its traffic; the traffic results from a lively city – a fact often forgotten by traffic planners. Transportation systems must be designed with an understanding of the totality of which they are a part. Unfortunately, most North American cities have not invested sufficient money, time or effort in building viable public transportation systems. The main reason is perhaps the difficulty municipalities have in securing financing.

Municipal taxation as presently practised in Canada is inadequate to distribute the financial load equitably. Property taxes form the basis of municipal income, but they cannot provide enough money to deal effectively with the many urban problems.

In Canada, municipalities obtain grants through federal and provincial sources. However, since the city has no direct control over these grants, and can only use them for certain purposes, cities can seldom plan effectively for their future. This is particularly true in transportation planning. For this reason, the car usually wins as it does not need the initial costly infrastructures required by a public transit system. However, in the long-term financial view of a city, the car is not the most efficient mode of urban transportation.

Many years ago a great public debate raged in Toronto about the efficiency of its public transportation system, and ways and means to prevent it from losing money. Professor Hans Blumenfeld, one of the consultants, suggested that fares be eliminated. The press broke out in laughter. However, from the standpoint of a city's economy, this could be a logical solution.

The Toronto Transit Commission (T.T.C.) spends approximately 15 per cent of its operating budget on the collection of fares. Eliminating fares would achieve an immediate 15 per cent reduction in operating costs. But in the long term, T.T.C. subways, streetcars and buses can carry passengers without further costs if the public would only use them. Increased use of existing T.T.C. facilities, due to eliminated fares, would then also reduce the need to expand other transportation systems, mostly roads.

If there were no fares, how would the Commission have money to operate with? Very simply, through taxation, the same way sidewalks, streets and all highways are paid for. The T.T.C. subway system is, in fact, little else but a rolling sidewalk. And nobody talks of a sidewalk losing money.

Subway Systems: Suited for High Densities

Subway systems were introduced into cities in the 19th century. We have lived with their benefits and shortcomings for nearly one hundred years.

The subway came into being to resolve transportation problems in the compact city that emerged towards the end of the last century. Modern subways have a passenger capacity of approximately 40000 riders per hour in each direction. Great densities in urban population are needed for them to operate efficiently, a condition that not all cities can meet, particularly in their suburbs. Modern cities seldom have the required densities outside their downtown cores and thus must have secondary feeder systems of streetcars, buses, cars or trains. However, such transfer systems are not as attractive to riders as direct, one-vehicle systems are.

The greatest competitor of all public transportation systems is the car. The convenience of door-to-door delivery has lured the modern city into nearly destroying itself. The space devoured by cars is staggering; they leave less and less land for other urban activities. Cities that have provided only for car transportation have transmuted themselves into suburban conglomerations, inimical to pedestrian life.

Unfortunately, merely recognizing the destructive action of the car on the city does not necessarily create a solution. In order to lure people away from car use and into public transportation systems, it is necessary to re-structure the urban environment so that it can work in conjunction with its transit system. For example, use of a public transit system declines if the distance from home or office to transit stop is much greater than 300 metres. In other words, intense density is essential for a subway system to exist.

63, 64
Peter Kwantes
Diagram for parking utilization in complex containing retail, office, and residential facilities.
Distance progressed on foot and by car

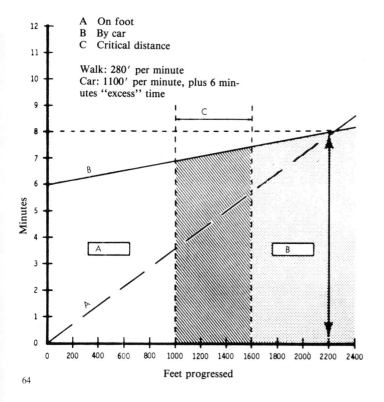

A   On foot
B   By car
C   Critical distance

Walk: 280′ per minute
Car: 1100′ per minute, plus 6 minutes "excess" time

Minutes

Feet progressed

64

However, despite such required density to have sufficient riders in close proximity to each station, since any transportation system is linear and nodal, both stations and adjacent transportation links can be built far enough apart to create open park spaces between them. This allows the use of such park systems immediately adjacent to dense urban areas and creates a better living environment within the urban area, without sacrificing the high-nodal density necessary for public transit to exist. This is, of course, contrary to the present North American practice of spreading densities equally over large urban areas and requires a coordination between transportation and living which, unfortunately, has been mostly left to chance in the past.

Intermediate Transportation Systems: Suited for Lower Densities

The great hope of the last decades was to develop intermediate transportation systems that could operate efficiently in densities lower than those required by subways. It is astonishing that not one of the many promising systems invented has been able to do this. Despite fantastic technological developments such as air-cushions, monorails, magnetic levitations and so forth, little has been translated into our everyday working reality up until now. Such systems are either too expensive to develop, or cities are unwilling or unable to accept the planning limitations necessary for including them in their urban fabric.

Most transportation networks need a system of right of ways to function effectively. Cities are seldom planned with such systems in mind. Normally a city's plan is based on its historic development and cannot easily adjust to modern transit requirements. Because the "old" streetcar could use the existing historic network, it has survived with surprising stamina. A lesson to learn from this is that even in transportation, overspecialization – as necessary in new, highly specialized systems – can lead to a dead-end.

At the moment, streetcars and their related modes of light, rapid, intermediate transit systems appear to be the main contenders for mass movement – other than the expensive capital-intensive subway systems and the flexible but even more expensive car-oriented road systems. Buses and their variations – minibus, dial-a-bus and computer bus – have the advantage of being able to function within an existing infrastructure, ie., the road system, but are relatively expensive to operate. They also do not enjoy the same emotional acceptance by the public as rail-oriented systems as being reliable. It is perhaps the constant visual presence of the rail that gives the emotional assurance that the train or tram will arrive in due course.

The Horizontal Elevator

One possibility not yet explored is the horizontal elevator that, like the vertical elevator, would only serve a limited area, yet would tie that area into other transportation systems. Such an elevator system could be constructed in sections, as needed within a city, and thus would have the flexibility that city areas, increasing in density, require.

Such systems are merely a logical extension of the vertical elevator system. Within some office complexes, up to 10000 people and more are moved daily from floor to floor via vertical elevators. Similar numbers can be moved from point to point by horizontal elevators. The horizontal movement system could resemble one of the many existing systems presently used at fairs. Such horizontal systems would be relatively short and would operate only in parts of the downtown. They would connect major activity centres to each other and to public transit stops. Urban districts served by horizontal elevators would have parking garages on their fringes also linked by these elevators. This would make it possible to keep cars outside such sections and return the street to the pedestrian. Extremely dense city areas served by such horizontal elevators could create the most efficient and economical system of urban transportation now available.

Parking Cars in Cities

No matter how efficient or attractive public transit is made, we still have to deal with the car. One difficulty is the transition of the automobile passenger into a pedestrian. This transfer from rider to pedestrian is done quite simply, using relatively little space, by a public transit system in streetcar stops or subway stations. Toronto's Queen Street subway station can handle 40000 people daily in 2300 square metres. Parking garages, however, need 37 square metres per car. With each car yielding an average of 1,4 pedestrians, over one million square metres would be required to handle the same number of people! This is nearly 230 times the space, not even considering the road space consumed by moving cars.

65

A further problem of parking places of cars is the inconsistent usage. Most garages serving office complexes are occupied only during business hours, giving roughly 35 % overall occupancy. Similar under-use exists for parking facilities serving other uses such as shopping or residential.

Diagram 64 shows how multi-use buildings with the proper mixture of functions could increase use of parking space. But even further improvements can be made. By incorporating parking with public transit links and multi-use buildings at the fringes of the dense downtown core, a far more efficient use of urban space could be achieved.

Cars must be kept somewhere, but car storage has seldom been solved satisfactorily in the downtown situation. The transitions between the stored car, public transportation and the city space have seldom been critically evaluated. To just stuff cars below street level and then to bring people out of these dungeons is not the best way to deal with car storage. Toronto's Eaton Centre exemplifies how orientation and connection of the parking space with the destination can be imaginatively dealt with. There, the parking elevators are placed inside the shopping galleria. Immediately upon entering the parking elevator lobby, the galleria is visible. Glass elevators further help people to orientate themselves.

Walking: The Most Important Mode of Urban Transportation

Walking is the basic method of urban traffic. Only as pedestrians can we perceive our environment without the distortions or warping created by speed. Only pedestrians can directly interact with our cities and in this way enrich them. If urban areas do not provide an environment conducive to pedestrians, then the life of the city is endangered. In too many places the pedestrian has been pushed away and the street turned into a raceway for cars, devoid of other attractions.

There are rules that can help create a good environment for pedestrians, rules that reflect human behaviour. First, streets are only successful if they provide a need for people to be on them. They must either furnish the actual destination points, such as theatres, department stores or shops, or they must be on the way to those or similar attractions. Second, urban spaces must be designed to have their activities along their edges. People always like to be with their backs towards a wall – looking towards the centre. People do not sit in the middle of a space if they can avoid it. Their first choice is the edge of a space with a building as protection behind them. For this reason, the Parisian sidewalk café is so successful. Third, since people like to see and be seen, the edges must be so designed that people being there can both see the passing pedestrians and be seen by them. Another most important element is the bench to rest on, to pull your child's socks up, to figure out what to do next, etc. And, fifth, pedestrian areas must be conceived as coherent urban spaces with clear orientation points, such as towers or monuments for example.

The palette of possibilities is nearly unlimited. We can use as models the wide Parisian street that successfully mixes pedestrians with cars, the totally pedestrian-orientated street as in the *Fußgängerzone* in Munich, the enclosed walkways of the Milan Galleria and the Parisian Passages, the small *Gassen* in Salzburg, or streets that border parks as found in Edinburgh's Princess Street. All these and more can be successful, but they can also turn into failures if the guidelines for creating good pedestrian spaces have not been adhered to.

The multi-use buildings that form the edge of such urban areas must acknowledge these rules and design spaces and activities to respond to them. They must respond with a visual complexity to the probing eye of the pedestrian, particularly at the street level, for at walking speed, the pedestrian can see detail, discover intimate visual spaces and requires visual stimulus. Higher speeds present fewer visual problems, since the faster the speed of traversing a space, the fewer details are perceived. Even rather ugly cities acquire beauty when viewed from the distance of a fast-moving airplane.

65
E. H. Zeidler
Eaton Centre, Toronto
Elevators from parking levels used as
orientation device

66
People using edges vs. centre

67
University Avenue, Toronto
Few pedestrians are encouraged

The Street

A city contains many types of streets. Each has its own meaning: there are bustling shopping streets, monumental streets expressing the power of institutions, quiet residential streets, and so on. Problems arise when a street has no meaning and no secondary role within the urban fabric.

Rudolphski wrote that "streets are for people" and questioned the North American attitude of giving the car preference. Unless people are attracted to and fascinated by a street, they will seldom use it. That is why many "pedestrian streets" are devoid of people. A good example is Toronto's stately University Avenue that barely ever sees a pedestrian just out for a stroll. Though everything is planned for him, it is done incorrectly. There are no shops to attract people, nothing but imposing offices or public buildings to rush in and out of on business. There is no reason to dally or saunter, especially since the car exhaust fumes burn in one's throat. Few people use the beautifully landscaped walkway scattered with fountains, flowers and bushes because it is isolated between two always busy roadways. People must go out of their way to reach the benches and gardens by crossing heavy traffic.

The pedestrian street must not be conceived as only a corridor that connects point A with point B, but also as an event. All the ingredients of a street must be skillfully arranged to achieve this – the way in which storefronts face the street, the way in which restaurants participate in street life, the way in which trees are set out and rest places are located.

The main boulevards of Paris provide many valuable lessons on how to build good city streets. The sidewalk café participates with the street and provides it with both an audience and a theatre. One augments the other: the pedestrian who walks by is diverted by the café's activity, and the restaurant patron inside still feels part of the city life.

Cars do not necessarily require banishment from the urban street as long as they dont domineer it. Introducing the car into city streets need not create conflict. Paris lives reasonably well with its cars, and at times even extremely successfully. Cars in cities provide their occupants not only with transportation but with entertainment as well. The particularly North American phenomenon which we could call the "Saturday Night Syndrome" exemplifies this. Here the car is not only a mode of transportation but also a means of amusement and exploration. In such roles the introduction of automobiles into the pedestrian environment, if skillfully handled, can enhance the life of the street.

The Square

The square or plaza as an urban space is actually an extension of the street, yet it is a node of special significance. In many cases the square is related to the symbolic meaning of the city. In times past, city squares were the *loci* of arrival for travellers and the places of public rituals. Vestiges of these functions survive in many civic squares and plazas.

Madrid's Plaza Reale or Toronto's City Hall Square are two urban spaces that successfully encourage participation. Particularly in Toronto, Viljo Revel's design for the City Hall Square achieved astonishing results despite a hostile surrounding of undefined streets and buildings. A raised walkway gives this huge square a visual enclosure, and a fountain pool/skating rink makes the vast square active not only during major public celebrations but on every day, winter or summer.

Despite such occasional successes, modern architecture has had problems in dealing with civic spaces. Since buildings were conceived as individual monuments, the urban form that civic spaces could achieve with these buildings was largely ignored by modern architects.

Le Corbusier's Ville Radieuse had no plazas, no enclosed squares. Space was left over. Buildings were designed to fulfill their individual meaning. They were sculptures, pieces of furniture, things that had relevance only to themselves.

The office tower, the apartment building, the shopping centre were never conceived as a link within an urban continuum. The possibility of compromising their individual function to achieve such urban integration was rejected by modern architects because it appeared to entail a loss of efficiency. But such loss is in fact imaginary if it is considered within the economy of the city.

Enclosed Walkways

Within cities the open street is still the best artery, regardless of the climate. There are, however, notable exceptions that also serve urban needs well. The enclosed passages built in the 19th century, like the magnificent Milan Galleria and the forgotten Cleveland Galleria, worked excellently.

68

69

70

Another direction in enclosed passages started in Montreal and was taken over by Toronto. Here a network of underground pedestrian walkways was created. Toronto will eventually have more than one and a half miles of them connecting subway stations, railway terminals, major buildings and over six hundred shops.

Such environmentally-controlled malls are practical in climates where weather conditions make half the year uncomfortable for pedestrians to be outside. However, the effect of these underground malls on the urban scene has not been fully evaluated.

If we decide to relegate people to underground malls by building the major attractions and the easiest circulation routes there, then our streets may only be capable of serving as transportation arteries for cars. If that is what we want, then we must make our choice and accept the consequences. But I believe the past has shown that this is not the best solution. There is a need for underground passages, but outside streets and urban spaces should not be neglected in their favour. The enclosed mall should not strangle other city spaces but must instead relate to them visually and physically, providing a choice for pedestrians of being outside or inside. This blending and mutual reinforcement of alternate environments not only strengthens the life of the city but also makes the mall more attractive. The Eaton Centre Galleria attempted such an integration of open street and day-lit mall.

Urban Political Structure

Buildings link together in chains and form cities. Each building must respect, reflect and reinforce the urban environment, which is affected by the static rules of urban space and the dynamic rules of urban movement patterns. But recognizing these rules and fulfilling them are two different things.

Implementation of these complex urban design rules depends greatly on the political structure under which an urban environment is created. Modern planning concepts have often ignored the political structure required to realize them. To implement Le Corbusier's Ville Radieuse would have certainly needed powers beyond those acceptable to any democratic society.

Cities: Reflections of Man's Social and Political Order

Man cannot live with others unless he accepts certain codes in his relationship with his fellow men. These ever-present codes are reflected not only in how he lives but also in the physical environment influenced and shaped by these codes. Therefore cities ultimately express the social and political structure that created them.

From antiquity on we can study such structures in the shells of cities. John Kenneth Galbraith listed four major city forms in "The Age of Uncertainty" that expressed changing political structures. These are the Political Household, the Merchant City, the Industrial City and finally the Suburb or Camp. Suburbs have no central political or economic function; they are but places of temporary domicile for the peripatetic modern man – hence the appellation "camp". Vestiges of all four are present in many cities of today.

The Political Household developed around the seat of power, either royal or religious. The city was an extension and representation of the magnificence of its being. Fatehpur Sikri, Angkor Wat, Versailles, Karlsruhe, Leningrad, Canberra and, in a strange way, Brasilia are prototypes of such cities. Their forms symbolically express the political power that created them. Order and symmetry even today are used to achieve such a representation of power.

The Merchant City also used order and coherence, yet in a less rigid form, to express the ruling style of the merchant class. Urban cohesion was created through the summation of many related parts, as exemplified by the houses of Amsterdam, Venice, as well as those of the Hanseatic cities that still bear witness to such an urban structure. The idea of downtown shopping is its legacy.

68
Nathan Phillip's Square
Successful urban space encouraging a variety of activities

69
Place de la Défense, Paris
Buildings as monuments fail to create urban space and its related activities

70
Piazza del Campo, Siena
The medieval urban space combining built form and urban activity

71

71
Milan Galleria

The Industrial Revolution created another kind of city, one that no longer felt it needed to express symbolically its political structure. Industrial cities, particularly in England, were used to house at lowest cost the other raw material needed for machines – the human operator.

Industrial cities fulfilled a demand of function. They occasionally struggled to find beauty by imitating bygone forms, such as apartment houses that attempted to resemble palazzos. Yet generally the industrial city took pride in its economic determination particularly in England where its prototype was developed and equated solidity and gracelessness with efficiency. The city was considered a mine that after the rich lode was taken out should be abandoned.

The fourth city type, the suburb, was created as an escape from the industrial city. It could only exist in conjunction with a city and had no meaning in itself. Suburbs became temporary abodes, yet through their magnitude they drastically changed the structure of the old city and created a non-city, the amorphous megalopolis.

Our seeming inability to create visually coherent cities today may be because we do not have a coherent social conception of our urban structure, thus lack a conviction to express it in an urban form and lack the political power to realize it.

Failure of Utopian and Modern Planning

Society's legal and political organization affects urban plans. Therefore we must not only consider technical planning solutions but also the political framework within which they will be realized.

Our present planning approach, particularly in North America, could be kindly described as a non-visual one. It is a two-dimensional engineering approach that has more in common with the estate game "Monopoly" than with an attempt to create environments fit for human beings. Modern planning theories have not created cities that are visually attractive to be in; on the contrary, voices condemning them are growing stronger. Confusion and isolation, clutter and monotony have created in many cities an atmosphere not only unpleasant but at times even damaging to the mental health of their inhabitants.

Failure of both the industrial city and the subsequent modern metropolis diverted some planners into utopian dreams that promised to resolve urban problems. Most utopian models attempted to create a new harmony between society and architectural form. These dreams of visionary unity started with Owen, St. Simon, Fourier, Ebenezer Howard, Le Corbusier and Frank Lloyd Wright; they continue today in the visions of Paolo Soleri.

Yet again and again over the last two centuries these visions have failed as realities because they, like all utopias, contain the seeds of self-destruction. More often, however, utopias cannot be realized since they entail changes so sweeping that only a totalitarian political system could enforce their creation – and such dictatorial power contradicts their basic concept of social equality.

The few utopian concepts that have been realized have not achieved what they promised but rather the opposite, a confined environment, ultimately static and dictatorial, that did not allow freedom for the individual.

Bryan Magee concludes in discussing Popper: "If you regard yourself as establishing the perfect society of the future, you will want to perpetuate this society when you get it. This will mean arresting the progress of change . . . by the most rigid social control: totalitarianism. This development is inherent from the beginning, though when it comes about, people will say that the theory has been perverted."

The Cultural Imprint: North America and Europe

The North American city is distinctly different from its European counterpart. Even though the suburbs of Paris and Toronto, or of any other North American city, may have a similar visual disorder, their cores differ. The reasons lie in the historical forces that built these two cultures.

The core of the European city developed through centuries and expresses bygone social organizations. The city form has imprinted itself into society, and is carried as a cultural heritage. This imprint of historicism fought against a takeover by modern planning, and resulted in compromises that preserved urban patterns.

North American experience was different. There was no strong cultural imprint of a past historic city. Most cities had little form other than the grid plan conceived by surveyors as an expedient method to divide land. The grid is the antithesis of symbolic expression in a city. It allows for few significant spaces,

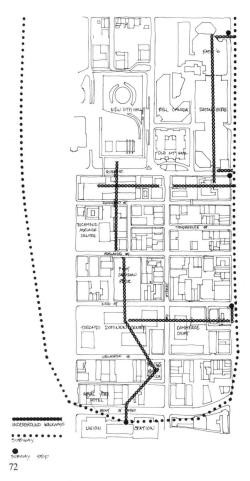

UNDERGROUND WALKWAYS
.... SUBWAY
● SUBWAY STOP
72

73

other than perhaps the urban parks introduced by the Olmsted movement. The only other variations are those caused by insurmountable topography.

The early American city was closer to the village in spirit, with single houses, free-standing churches and treelined avenues. The visual urbanity created by a dense urban condition was new in America, being imported with the 1893 Chicago World Fair by men like D. H. Burnham. Despite the fact that Daniel Burnham designed some of the first "Skyscrapers", when he had to deal with urban design he seemed to be unable to accommodate it and reverted back to the familiar massing of the European walk-up apartment form. Since he and others like him removed the historic American village precedents in the name of progress, it was only logical that in time their "city beautiful" would also be replaced with new, more progressive planning ideals. Unlike in Europe they found in America few historic precedents to stem their tide. Even the American skyscraper, perhaps with a few exceptions such as the Rockefeller Centre, did not find a way to express its urban potential before it was run over by the "anti-urban" modern ideals which in fact rejected urban density – yet created it through the back door of the potential land exploitation that they made possible.

America's Concept of Individual Freedom

North America, in contrast to Europe, has grown around an almost spiritual concept of individual freedom. People wanted to be unhampered by institutions. It was natural that this ideal of freedom was also expressed in attitudes towards land which was unfortunately transferred into urban land uses.

The ideal was not in conflict with the growth of villages, partly because America's early agrarian economy disciplined village expansion naturally. However, as society became more industrial and as ownership of vital urban land consolidated, this concept created conflict between the individual's right and the common good. However, by this time the individual's right to his land and its development potential had become equated with the spiritual concept of North American freedom. That is why modern planning theories that were against a coherent urban form and instead promulgated the unhampered expression of an individual building's function were readily accepted, as they went hand in hand with the idea of land as a commodity belonging to the individual.

Together these two ideas, the individual building and land as an individual commodity, led to the demise of the modern North American city.

In such an environment, planning restrictions and interventions were thought not only to be unnecessary but amoral and counter to the spirit of freedom. It was assumed that technology, free enterprise and progress would ultimately right any wrongs that might occur during urban growth.

The Danger of Progress for the Sake of Progress

Progress can totally wipe out part of a city's history. The number of magnificent Beaux Arts buildings destroyed in Toronto alone since the end of the Second World War is hard to imagine.

The euphoria of progress demands the destruction and subsequent reconstruction at greater densities of any building that is successful. The concept seems to be that if any building is successful, then its land value must be high, and thus a more successful building would create an even higher land value. The corollary to this is that unsuccessful buildings cannot be replaced because their land values are too low. Therefore, they remain dilapidated. This explains in part the immediate adjacency of the brand-new skyscraper and the dilapidated shack in American cities.

North American cities have become visual battlefields of constant urban growth and decay, largely for the sake of such rather ephemeral progress. Lack of building controls for their visual maintenance – other than fire and safety regulations for occupied buildings – have contributed to this decay. Cities in the process of free growth create sharply defined adjacencies of urban success and failure. This process is ultimately highly destructive for our cities and can only be prevented by changing our approach to planning. We must begin to consider our urban resources as limited and not boundless. We must prevent the destruction of good building stock merely because of the accident of ownership.

72
Toronto
Toronto system of underground walkways

73
Eaton Centre
Underground section. Open street and daylit mall

74
Canberra

75
Brasilia

process of free growth create sharply defined adjacencies of urban success and failure. This process is ultimately highly destructive for our cities and can only be prevented by changing our approach to planning. We must begin to consider our urban resources as limited and not boundless. We must prevent the destruction of good building stock merely because of the accident of ownership.

Presently we are acting like a young couple furnishing a living room without sufficient funds to buy all pieces at one time. So they augment their few good pieces with makeshift furniture. As funds arrive new pieces are bought, yet to the surprise of all, the makeshift furniture stays and the "good" furniture is replaced with more pretentious pieces.

Building a Visual Urban Framework

At present, North American urban planning controls are two-dimensional and do not deal with the reality of three-dimensional urban space. Therefore urban space no longer controls the visual environment but has become something left over after the fact.

Modern architects have always believed that the form of their buildings could be developed individually without reference to a formal urban fabric. It was thought wrong to predetermine the context of the urban space and thus limit the individual building. Such an attitude is still prevalent. The result of this attitude is the separation of planning from architecture. This means the planner deals with the two-dimensional aspects of land use unrelated to the urban space that will be the ultimate result. Urban planning is more than a two-dimensional affair of balancing functional relations; it includes the architectural design of three-dimensional urban spaces. Unfortunately, many modern architects rejected the existence of three-dimensional urban design, believing such design to be achievable through zoning legislation and individual design freedom. This has not been the case, and our cities have suffered accordingly.

Few North American urban designs show an independent but coherent framework in which different architects have developed their buildings. Of those that do, most complete an existing historic concept, like the Mall in Washington, D. C. In general, however, modern urban design has accomplished the opposite of an open but contiguous urban framework. Even the sculptural totality of such new pojects as Chandigarh does not contradict such judgement as it prohibits the freedom of independent, individual participation.

The urban plan for Pickering, near Toronto, is an attempt to create a framework that would allow for the growth of a coherent urban form with individual diversity. The concept is that such form can be realized through related but individual buildings, created by different architects. The various buildings, as they are designed, may adjust the overall concept, yet would do so with an understanding and perception of the final urban space which they will be part of.

Historic Parallels to a Visual Urban Framework

The architect who designs an individual building within any urban context can only do so successfully if he works within an existing urban context, or if the concept of the future urban form is defined. In the past prior to the modern movement, the urban framework was usually understood and most buildings were designed to adapt to it.

The coherence of historic urban spaces was seldom an accident. As early as 1609, Louis XIII created the Place des Vosges and reserved ownership of the axial pavilions for himself, in order to maintain a visual coherence. Between 1685 and 1699, Mansart designed the façades only of the Place Vendome and Place des Victoires for Louis XV in a similar way, with the individual owner filling in the rest.

76
Merchant city
Expression of merchant class as ruling
order through order and coherence

145

77

78

79

But Paris was not alone in such early planning. In 1764 and 1769, J. Wood designed the Circus and Royal Crescent in Bath, England. Regent's Park, designed by Nash in 1812, also followed the principle of creating a unified façade for a number of separate houses. Yet even the more romantic but still unified urban spaces of medieval cities were the result of laws – written and unwritten, including natural restrictions.

Yet despite the success of these early coherent urban designs, modern theories have abhorred such unity of exterior urban space. It was thought contradictory to architectural principles that demanded the expression of internal function truly and honestly in the external form. These principles mistakenly equate morality with formal expression. It is a misleading philosophy that equates truth with form and uses morality to defend a stylistic attitude. That form follows function is but a half truth. In Churchill's words, the reverse is also true, namely that an ordered framework may sustain a function.

The New Urban Democracy

Only by first seeing the failure of modern urban planning principles can we then attempt to create the political management needed to build successful, coherent urban frameworks. Such frameworks must be open in the sense that they allow individual participation and change, yet they must also be able to maintain a coherent urban environment through their three-dimensional context of space and activity. In maintaining freedom, one does not have to degenerate into chaos; in creating unity, one does not have to impose architectural dictatorship. This is the equivalent of an architectural democracy.

An architectural democracy has nothing in common with utopian architectural ideals. Karl Popper, in his book "The Open Society", rejects the utopian ideal of maximizing happiness, for in practice such an imaginary standard must result in intolerance and authoritarianism.

The most positive aspect of Popper's work is his theory that the greatest of all revolutions is the transition from a closed society into an open society. His open society would be an association of free individuals, respecting each other's rights within a framework of mutual protection supplied by the state. It would achieve, through the making of responsible, rational decisions, a growing measure of humane and enlightened life.

A social framework that permits compromises among its constituents allows maximum personal expression. Such a framework is not a kind of super being to which the individual owes servitude; rather it is the means of giving the individual minimum constraint.

We must plan our urban environment to best achieve such an open society. Urban design must not only give us a coherent, unified environment that responds to our physical and emotional needs; it must also give us the freedom to unfold as individuals. This dual need raises the old dichotomy of freedom and restriction. Yet in reality they are not in conflict, for ultimately, human freedom can only be achieved by understanding and accepting the discipline of life.

The framework I envisage for the city is the symbolic expression of visual order. Like Popper's open society, it is an open framework, one of reference and response to its surroundings. In addition, this visual framework must reflect not only our present reality but our cultural heritage as well. For to our amazement we are finding the ambience of the old type of city, with all its so-called unfunctionalism, more enjoyable than the modern city. This realization has created an undercurrent that is now coming to the surface and changing our concepts towards our cities. Unfortunately, history has taught us that there is always a considerable time lag between the emergence of a philosophical concept and its political realization. Perhaps we can shorten this time lag between thought and action.

77
Versailles

78
Industrial city
Finding beauty through imitating past forms. Apartments like palazzos

79
Minneapolis
Modern city. Nonvisual. Confusion

80
Suburb. Noncity. Amorphous mega lopolis

80

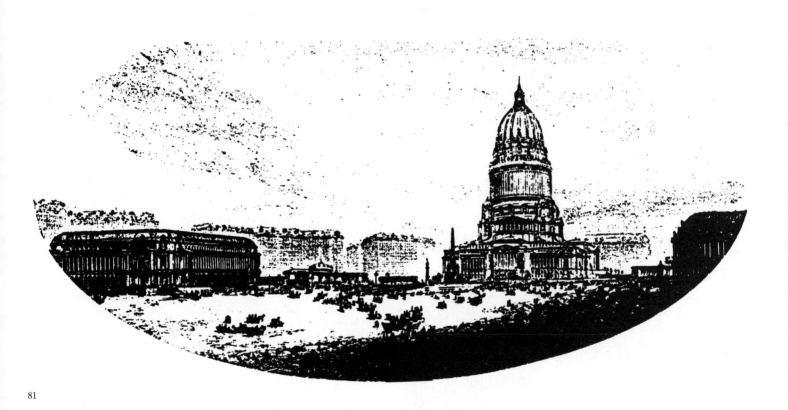

81

81
D. H. Burnham
Plan of Chicago. Proposed city centre
square

82

Emotional Demands

The way in which we perceive and react to our buildings makes them a human experience. Our emotional perception is more than a reaction, for it ultimately becomes a powerful force and we must understand it, if we want to design cities well-suited to human beings.

Emotional impact cannot be explained logically or scientifically, yet this seeming failure does not render the subject unimportant. On the contrary, the physical environment has a profound effect on human emotion, which in turn brings about a counter-effect on our man-made environment. Emotions generate in man the desire to have a particular type of environment, one that suits him. In discussing the forces that influence the multi-use building, we cannot omit emotions which demand an urban environment responsive to the needs of the human psyche in all its contradictions and complexities.

Emotional Demands: What They Are

The Oxford Dictionary defines emotion as "A mental feeling of affection as distinguished from cognition and volition". It encompasses feelings outside rational knowledge or conscious will.

Our emotional responses are governed by hidden subconscious programming that is the result of psychological, ethical and aesthetic influences; also related to the human psyche and its cultural background.

In 1970, Prohansky *et al*'s book, "Environmental Psychology", attempted to define a new science which studied man's psychological reaction to his environment, ordered and defined by him. Because man is both the victim and the conqueror of it, his ability to predict, even to a limited extent, the consequences of his environmental planning places a unique responsibility on him.

Simpson in 1966 suggested in "Science" that this ability is the biological basis for an ethical action, a moral imperative beyond the necessary condition of survival. I feel while both the psychological and the ethical reaction are very much a basis of the emotional demands influencing our environment, emotion in my interpretation encompasses more. It reaches also into the field of aesthetics.

Emotions not only react to questions of practical survival and moral issues, they also respond to mental images. An image is a mental representation of a physical form that has been changed into something not quite matching its objective reality by the mind of the beholder. Mental representations are influenced by many factors: the human psyche, previous experiences, historical precedence, cultural influences, etc. This process is a key factor in our perception of anything, our environment included. Thus the impact our surroundings have on us is strongly influenced by our emotional response to it.

The Emotional Effect of Urban Space

The urban environment affects human life more than we are presently capable or willing to admit, not only because we are limited in the scientific means to measure such effect, but also because this urban environment has grown to such magnitude that it nearly encompasses all of man's life. Modern man may feel he has many ways of escaping an engulfing, threatening urban space, but they are not as plentiful as he may think. The city dweller is enclosed most of the time in his man-made environment. With growing urbanization, more and more time will be spent in such surroundings.

Thus urban spaces must be evaluated for their human liveability and psychological functionalism, in the same way as individual buildings have been studied. Acceptance of an emotional criterion for the urban environment will change our attitude in planning individual buildings. The building's exterior form – its façade – can no longer remain an expression of only its interior functions; it must reflect a compromise between interior necessity and the exterior demands of the urban fabric. Both issues demand the consideration of emotions. Urban spaces affect man emotionally as much as the interior places he lives and works in. Exterior civic spaces are not merely the corridors between one destination and the next that modern planners thought them to be. They are places "to be" and live in, and as such they have meaning for man. Urban spaces must be designed to respond to man's emotional perception of it.

82
Place des Vosges, Paris
Coherent urban space designed as urban entity

83
Royal Crescent, Bath
Unified facade

84

85

emotions. Urban spaces affect man emotionally as much as the interior places he lives and works in. Exterior civic spaces are not merely the corridors between one destination and the next that modern planners thought them to be. They are places "to be" and live in, and as such they have meaning for man. Urban spaces must be designed to respond to man's emotional perception of it. The individual buildings are part of this response, because urban space is the summation of individual buildings.

Illusion and Urban Space

Urban space is subject to visual illusion and may be perceived differently from its actual physical reality. The blended image that results from an inhabitant's various snapshot perceptions will become his perceived reality of the city. Thus two cities having the same density may be perceived as having different densities. One city may appear to be enjoyable and filled with life, while the other may seem to be depressingly overcrowded. The different perceptions result from the physical ways in which density has been accommodated and the methods used affect the perceiver's emotions. We must accept that there is an interplay between physical urban form and human emotion.

But the physical manipulation of space is differently conceived depending on psychological, cultural, social and other influences that affect the urban image.

The same urban space will have different meanings to different people at different times. The reaction to urban space cannot always be predicted, nor can the beauty of an urban space be measured. We don't know how far an urban space is intrinsically beautiful or only is conceived so, through use and familiarity. But perhaps only the beautiful thing ultimately becomes familiar.

Despite man's changing emotional attitudes, there exist some pragmatic guidelines for creating pleasing urban spaces. Logic does not seem to control these guidelines but if they are ignored, the total urban space is often ineffective.

The illusion of urban space is subject to proportion, continuity, complexity, materials and so forth, similar rules that control art and architecture. The Piazza of St. Peter in Rome by Bernini and the vast screen-type façade by Maderna that obscures Michelangelo's original Greek cross, indicate how the use of proportions changed in scale, can create spatial illusions that defy the reality of space.

Urban space must interrelate the perception of its physical form, not only with the needs of its human activities, but also with the illusion of such life. A plaza may be surrounded with all kinds of human activities, but if they are not visible, such urban space may appear dead.

Even the most seemingly simple urban space is intrinsically complex. Yet often only in retrospect do we discover this complexity, mostly through the negative of omission do we realize the missing ingredient necessary to effective urban space.

Our Emotional Contact with the Past

As we gain greater freedom through technology to experiment with urban form, we appear to have lost the unity in our man-made environment that older technologies naturally imposed. Medieval cities, because of limited building materials, usually worked with only a few elements which had limited ranges of application. For example, certain areas had only clay available for roof tiles and these had to be installed in a predetermined slope. Precisely these restrictions created a formal unity in medieval cities that is still unsurpassed. The apparent freedom we have achieved today through technology, with its vast choice of materials and techniques, seems to result in visual chaos. Urban structures that have achieved visual success are those to which an artificial discipline has been applied.

The visual coherence of Hausmann's Parisian boulevards results from a discipline of necessity, though of another kind. Building heights were then limited to a certain number of floors because elevators had not yet been invented. In order to achieve maximum land usage, buildings of uniform height were constructed. This created the Parisian street's coherent urban space that we still admire. To achieve such visual unity today, disipline must be artificially introduced and maintained.

While such restraint would be condoned today, the nagging question remains: Is urban space created through imposed discipline attractive to us only because we are familiar with these forms? Or could we change our preference for such historic precedents and use our technology to create new urban spaces outside established patterns that ultimately would have equal emotional appeal to us?

84
TD Centre
Combination of modern functionalism with German classicism

85
Schinkel, Altes Museum

149

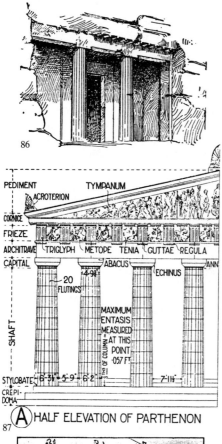

86

(A) HALF ELEVATION OF PARTHENON

87

88   89

Modern Architecture's Failure to Provide for Emotional Demands

The first attempts to achieve a totally new urban pattern failed. Modern architecture endeavoured to determine the city's form by complying only to the demands of urban functional needs, denying historic forms their continued reality. In the theory of functionalism, historic forms were merely expressions of past functions and therefore meaningless if repeated today, since the functions and construction methods that created these forms were outdated.

History, human emotion, and our resulting cultural heritage do not respond to such logic. Today's architects are re-evaluating their attitude towards these issues. We are now realizing that no form is ever new but is, in Koestler's word, a "bisociation" of past memories. "Bisociation" denotes the new event that results when two known events are associated in a hitherto unknown way. Even Mies van der Rohe's stark Toronto-Dominion Centre is an example of such bisociation. It combined in a new form modern functionalism and the German Classicism which had its roots in Greek architecture.

Transmutation of Functional into Emotional Form

In the evolution of architectural form, functional elements have always become transmuted into formal elements. These formal elements, detached from their original functional task, took on meanings which had only an emotional connection with their previous use. Often even this connection was lost and a totally new meaning became attached to the formal configuration.

Already classical Greek architecture exemplifies this transmutation from functional to purely emotional form. The Doric order contains, in all its details, the formalized remnants of wooden construction. The *triglyph* represents the formal ending of long-gone crossbeams, and the *guttae* the memory of wooden pegs that held the beams in place. Yet these transmuted emotional forms have been haunting Western civilization for over two thousand years! Adapting and changing these patterns to new uses, Palladio's 16th Century transmutations foreshadowed those of Classicism and their eventual change into Victorian cast-iron forms. Even today these past forms are enjoying a surprising resuscitation.

Why do these formal elements of classical Greek architecture have such lasting influence? All explanations based on structural, formal or cultural levels touch only part of their total reality; their basic strength lies in their emotional power over us.

Multi-Use Buildings in Urban Setting

Buildings are not only entities by themselves but are also part of the urban setting. The reality of an individual building and our perception of it within an urban context can be quite different. The emotionally perceived reality of a building can be changed drastically without substantially changing the nature of that building. For example, an office tower right on the street can dwarf that street and its pedestrians with an awesome, superhuman height. But this height can be obscured by putting a low building in front of the tower, thereby establishing a human scale street-scape.

The Yonge Street façade of Toronto's Eaton Centre is an example of maintaining the integrity of a street space by illusion. The predominantly three-storey strip character of Yonge Street was accepted and reflected in a front façade that maintains the street's generally uniform height. Stepping back the higher mass of the Eaton Centre keeps it from intruding into the established street space.

The Eaton Centre's western façade, though different, also fulfills the principle of respecting its urban setting. Here the Centre abuts a historical square surrounding a small church, the Holy Trinity. The overwhelming mass of the Eaton Centre was scaled down through steps on this side to a height lower than the church's eaves. Trinity Square development abuts the same square and continues the eaves' height with a two-storied arcade enclosing the square. The

86
Formalised remnants of past construction, already present in protodoric columns of Beni Hasan. Middle Empire (2160–1788 B.C.)

87
Greek temple, showing triglyph and guttae

88
Palladio

89
Soho, New York
Victorian cast iron

90

higher housing component of the Trinity Square development is set back so that it will not interfere. As seen by a pedestrian standing in the square, the church has now been transformed through the visual illusion of the lower arcade from a small object that was dominated by its towering neighbours into the visual focus that commands the square. The urban environment here was changed from a summation of isolated buildings to a continuum of urban events and spaces that are related to each other.

The City as an Artform

A city is negative architecture. If the interior spaces enclosed by a physical building express architecture, then the exterior urban spaces enclosed by individual buildings are created by the reverse or negative sense of architecture. Therefore, a city is not its buildings as isolated entities, but the urban spaces formed by parts of the buildings. Unfortunately, often all that modern architecture has done for the art of city design is to have leftover spaces between buildings.

Modern architecture never accepted, that city building is an art that must be conceived beyond a mere functional level. Even today few writers concerned with city planning concede that beyond a city's functional, economic and social importance is a level in which the city becomes an artform. Even less would they admit it as an *a priori* condition, though some may acknowledge it as being an *a posteriori* condition. This latter viewpoint would contend that urban forms are there because they happened, and since they are there we have come to like them, and because we like them, we consider them an artform.

Art, like life, is based on a material existence, yet it is the expression of the human spirit that rises above such earthbound materialism.

We are short-changing our lives by insisting that the city is not an artform. We react visually and emotionally to a city just as much as we do to a piece of art. Indeed, art expresses the human spirit, and the art of city building should reflect this.

City planning is expressed in urban space. Urban space transcends the individual architectural elements that create its form. Since all form evokes emotional reactions in man, a value judgement of like or dislike towards the city is automatically produced. Such value judgement is also influenced by personal or cultural codes. For this reason, architectural forms that differ from established patterns need time to become accepted.

Modern architectural forms discarded historic forms. The logic of functionalism and the quasi-logic of the moral value of truth in architectural expression were used to establish modern forms as the only acceptable ones. It was argued that form should be shaped only by social, functional and constitutional forces. But man is guided not only by his logical conscious mind but also by his emotions which reach up from the subconscious.

The limited range of modern architectural forms was caused by the denial of emotions' independent power to create form.

Emotions are notoriously inarticulate and often incommunicable in verbal terms, yet their existence cannot be denied.

Papez-MacLean triune brain model that establishes the independence of emotions created in the limbic system is not the full explanation of such division between subconscious emotions and conscious reasoning.

The division of left and right hemispheres in the cerebral neocortex – with the left controlling rational, computational functions and the right controlling intuition, vision and pattern recognition – further complicates the matter. This lack of integration in our brain between the rational and the emotional increases our inability to verbally express what man requires emotionally from his environment.

Man seems to find a mental calmness in contemplating nature. But his recent

91

92

90
Low building in front of tower integrates higher building with established street height

91
Low buildings toward Fifth Avenue relate centre to streetscape

92
E. H. Zeidler
Eaton Centre, Yonge Street facade
Illusion of three story strip character

93

94

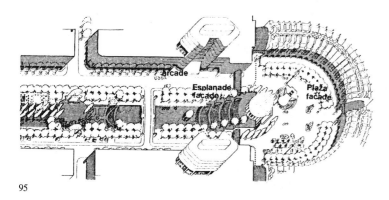

95

man-made environment seldom has created a similar mental calmness. More often the reverse is true and a feeling of jarring disharmony is produced.

Art theories in the past tried to set down absolute rules for the creation of harmony in forms. They did not succeed, even though some of their theories have had a strong influence on us. And yet rules of harmony exist that have validity. These rules are tied into man's ability to intuitively perceive order, symmetry, complexity, balance and contrast. Yet they are not absolute and their validity is subject to cultural changes. Polyclitus created in the Doryphorus the Canon of Greek sculpture, rules that had great influence yet were not universal to all cultures.

Successful cities and urban spaces are designed; they don't just happen. The great cities of the past are planned even though in retrospect some appear not to be. The complexity of Medieval cities, the intricate relationship of street hierarchies, vistas, towers and monuments, the visual length of spaces scaled to the pedestrian – all of these things did not happen by accident. Of course, they have nothing in common with the monotonous engineering concepts that today are equated with planning, but they were certainly planned in the sense that their inhabitants had definite ideas on how to integrate their individual buildings into a visual, harmonious whole.

The visual completeness of these cities of the past is much admired today. We can only achieve such an urban continuum again if we are willing to accept urban design guidelines that establish the ways in which urban space can grow. I am talking here of guidelines that accept the Collage nature of a city, guidelines that link the many complexities and contradictions of a city into a coherent form, not a giant geometry that would ultimately only add monotony. However, no North American city has yet accepted this concept.

Art and Life

Being successful as art however does not ensure success as an urban space. This requires that human activity be present also. For illustration, an interesting comparison can be found in Haussmann's Parisian boulevards, in Paris' Place de la Defence, and in some of Madrid's boulevards built before the turn of the century. Each of these deal with urban space and human activities in different combinations, but only the first was totally successful.

Haussmann's boulevards created a continuous street form lined with shops. These shops and their easy access drew that vital ingredient: human activity. On the other hand, the modern Place de la Defence had no developed, unified form. It consisted of monofunctional buildings, isolated sculptures, set in a park atmosphere. Although it has shops, hotels, restaurants, offices, residences and subways, it failed to be successful because it lacked an urban space that created a visual environment which encouraged human activities to unfold. Madrid's Victorian streets have a coherent urban street form, but shops and restaurants were removed from it as though in fear commercialism would diminish the street's dignity and defile its beauty. While visually delightful, it lacked human activity and failed as a successful urban space. Only Haussmann's boulevards had both key elements – form and activity. That is why his streets endured.

Urban Design in Search of Acceptance

Our failure to create excellent urban design is not due to our inability to deal with its problems, artistically or technologically. The reason is simple: we have convinced ourselves that cities should not be designed as coherent art forms. The argument that insists society cannot unfold in a planned environment is true if we understand coherent design to be barrack-like rigidity. But this is not the coherence I mean. A visually coherent urban design should be full of complexity and integrate many thoughts. It should create a city full of different collages.

The economic argument says cities cannot be designed because they must be free to respond to market forces. Behind this argument lurks the concept that urban land is a private commodity to be exploited at maximum value. The greatest benefit for the greatest number is not served by such economic reasonings.

I am not arguing here from a socialist position, but from a Keynesian one. He said in 1938 that "Economics is essentially a moral science". Keynes believed in liberal capitalism for moral reasons. He thought that the destruction of economic freedom ultimately would lead to the demise of political freedom. He came from economic reasoning to a similar position which Karl Popper philosophically arrived at. In "Democracy and Efficiency" (1939), Keynes looks for ". . . a system in which we can act as an organized community for common purposes, and promote social and economic justice, while respecting and protecting the individual – his freedom of choice, his faith, his mind and its impression, his

93
Haussmann's Parisian boulevards
Successful integration of urban space
and urban activity

94
Place de la Défense, Paris
Lacking urban space prohibits unfolding of urban activities

95
Pickering

96
Madrid boulevard
Not totally successful

enterprise and his property". Urban design is such an act of an organized community for common purposes.

All successful urban spaces, past or present, express a certain spirit, through continuity and coherence, to which we respond emotionally. Subordinating individual buildings to the emotional urban context is as important as providing for their functional requirements. Ultimately urban space transcends function and becomes art that speaks to us on another level – that of the spirit.

The introduction of Cartesian philosophy into Western thinking brought an explosion of scientific thought, a new understanding of the world and how to manipulate it. But this scientific thought also amputated an important aspect of our lives – the spiritual dimension. Attempts to only fulfill a city's functional and economic necessities stifled its emotional and spiritual growth. It reached the point where anything that could not be quantitatively assessed had no relevance in modern town planning. This limitation can be overcome only if we understand a city's emotional impact on its inhabitants and plan for it. Urban life and the buildings that support it cannot unfold in all its richness if this dimension is eliminated from our cities.

A Mandate

Manifestos have gone out of style. They seemed to belong to a past period that enjoyed adopting a heroic stance. We experienced the results of such "heroism" in the early part of this century and look now for less definite statements.

Yet at times I think we must commit ourselves so that events are not allowed to take place which may prove to be irreversible.

Past experience has shown that we must change our approach to the city. Progress, technology, economy and the tremendous changes they have brought are not goals in themselves that can be considered in isolation. On the other hand, man and his psychological reaction to his enviroment has changed little over the centuries.

Today many must live the majority of their lives in an urban environment, yet we have lost the art of creating it for him. Not only have we lost the art to do it, but also the confidence that we can do so.

We must plan and yet we do not believe in planning. We need order, yet we reject it because it reminds us of regimentation. We believe in freedom of architectural expression, in pluralism, in inclusiveness, and our urban environment has become a visual chaos. We shudder at the ultimate order that Fascist planning, the vision of a plan Voisin or an Arcology have in store for us; and yet we need an urban order, a framework in which the individual can unfold and change, which is expressed by a visual coherence.

I envisage this framework not as the inflexible skeleton of a technological megastructure, but as a mental concept of urban discipline. Of course it must be related to our physical and psychological reality as well as our technological infrastructure. Within such urban framework we need an interchangeable building block to realize such urban environment. I consider the multi-use building to be one of those building blocks, as it contains within itself the complexity of urban life and the ability to integrate, adjust and change within the urban fabric.

But to be such an urban building block, the multi-use building should follow certain rules that, taken as a whole, embody the urban dichotomy: the relation of the building to its urban situation and also to its own needs.

Therefore multi-use buildings should:

– Conserve Urban Space

A city can only create freedom of choice through concentration and density. Density is not directly related to the quality of space that is created. The same density may create in one case a totally enjoyable environment while, in another case, it may create unbearable conditions, but urban life is unthinkable without density.
The external, natural environment must be brought into balance with the needs of the built form: e.g., some spaces need sun penetration and daylight, and others do not.

Multi-use buildings are capable of providing, by interfacing various space uses, optimum conditions for each at maximum densities.
The multi-use building could prevent the waste of urban space, such as open parking lots, unused roof areas of low structures, etc. Through its proper use sunlight could enter where it should and allow open green spaces related to its urban use.

– Relate to and Create Urban Activity

The ambiance of a city is determined by the urban activities that it provides and how they relate to its public spaces. Urban activities are in fact limited in their number and must be carefully handled in order not to be wasted. Removing these public activities from areas where they are visible into hidden private spaces ultimately will reduce the livability of a city. It is therefore important to encourage the multi-use building not only to place its uses which relate to public activities in such a way as to maximize their accessibility and visibility, but also to encourage the introduction of such activities that help to maintain the life of the city. These urban activities may vary from shopping to sitting in a park, but they all relate to the overall network of the city.

– Be a Link within the Urban Space

Urban buildings are not sculptures within themselves, except in isolated cases, but are part of a greater whole. The majority of multi-use buildings must accept their role as visual and functional links within the urban form. The façade and its response to the urban space becomes again an issue. Our recognition and understanding of a city is through its urban spaces, streets, squares, etc., which are in turn created by the linked façades of individual buildings.

– Foster Social Dispersion

A by-product of growth seems to be the expulsion of unfamiliar elements. The ultimate result of this process is the ghettoization of the city and its inherent problems.

Such takeover or confinement of one group in an urban district appears to be a natural process of growth. In its early stages, perhaps, it is a healthy one, because people like to be with their own kind. However, if such growth is allowed to go unchecked, it leads to the Pruit-Igoe syndrome and the decay of a city. It is essential to maintain an urban social balance. The multi-use building can help to maintain such a necessary fine-grained social pattern.

– Relate to the Historic and Cultural Situation of its Place

Like a river, life is on-going. Yet we can only understand it if we have a fixed point to which we can relate the movement.

Architecture is the expression of the culture of a people – past and present, and buildings become the shells of such past culture.

Cities are for our life today and should not be a museum; but by totally erasing the past we may also destroy our future.

The multi-use building must accept its part as a building block in such cultural continuum. It must accept the existing urban situation and at times this may even require to fit within the shell of a historic building, or the continuation of a historic façade. Each urban building must recognize the historic and cultural condition of its site; the way in which this is done is the Art of Architecture.

– Respect the Needs of each Individual Function

The ultimate fulfillment of functions was the credo of modern architecture. Form follows Function was its battle cry. In realizing the shortcomings of such theory we must avoid replacing it with an equally simplistic slogan as supplied by Peter Blake: Form follows Fiasco. Neither was this modern theory all wrong, nor did it express the whole truth.

Any function will require a certain space to live within; however, function does not need to be taken as the only generator for the architectural expression of its form. To a degree, functions can adjust to many forms, however there are cases where a particular form can give optimum physical, psychological or economic fulfillment to a particular function.

A certain living unit or working space may require specific conditions such as perhaps a view, cross ventilation, moisture or shade. These are not ultimate rules, but only individual ones that relate to a particular need. Yet they must be respected and the urban system must allow their fulfillment.

– Inter-relate the Various Different Functions

It is important that not only the requirements of the individual's function are fulfilled, but also that the inter-related needs of functions are considered.

A restaurant close to living units is advantageous for a residential area; but the restaurant also needs working places close-by to have a noon trade. This simplistic example indicates the complexity of functional inter-relation. Such joining of functions – commercial activities related to residential units, living related to work areas, etc. – within close proximity, creates an urban synergetic action that multi-use buildings can achieve.

– Optimize Technology

Our enthusiasm for having discovered that today we still can find meaning in the past is no reason to turn the clock of architecture back and pretend there are no new forms. While it is ludicrous to design a city in the form of a lunar space module, it is equally absurd to make a space frame look like a stone temple. The exploration and the integration of new technological forms into our architectural vocabulary is an ongoing process that we cannot prevent. Much of the impetus of modern architecture came from a pent-up process that denied new technological forms their rightful place. However, the reverse situation occured in modern architecture, where past forms were denied their rightful place just because they were historic. The multi-use building must freely respond to modern technology; not as a formal expression but as a practical necessity.

– Achieve Economy

It is easy to establish the initial capital cost of a building, it is not so easy to evaluate its operating and maintenance cost, to evaluate its so-called life cycle costing. Yet it becomes more difficult to evaluate the adaptation cost, that is the cost to change the building after one functional cycle is completed and the next one begins. In health science buildings within a few decades such an adaptation cost can be several times the initial capital cost.

Yet it is most difficult to evaluate the economy of a building within the context of a city. Finally, true economy is only achieved if all four levels are being inter-related: capital, operating, maintenance and adaptation costs.

Building capital, maintenance and energy costs are very much related to each other and it is in this sense that I would like to look at energy – not in the simplistic narrow sense in which we consider it today under the slogan of energy conservation. There are prize winning energy efficient office buildings that are used between 9 and 4:40 on weekdays only, otherwise they stand empty 70% of the time. The workers arrive there by cars that burn more energy than the building. This is the wrong approach to energy saving. The multi-use building can bring about a new level of economy in the total life cycle cost, not only within the building but also within the urban fabric.

– Respond to the Human Psyche

The urban spaces created by individual buildings and their façades, as well as the interior spaces of these buildings react on the human psyche. This emotional response is beyond a logical explanation based on functional, structural or economic considerations; yet perhaps it is the strongest reaction that we experience in our physical environment. There are measurable psychological reactions that within certain limitations can be assessed. A new science "Environmental Psychology" has developed in the hope of expanding our understanding. Yet there is a level of psychological reaction to our environment that is immeasurable. We must find expression in our buildings for a response to it, individually and as part of the urban space. The multi-use building, because it is part of architecture, must finally transcend the level of functional reaction and respond to the search of meaning in our life.

Bibliography

Banham, Reyner: Megastructures, New York 1976
– The New Brutalism. Ethic or Aesthetic?, London 1966
Benevelo, Leonardo: The Origins of Modern Town Planning, Cambridge 1971
Le Corbusier: The Athens Charter, New York 1973
– Looking at City Planning, New York 1971
– Towards a New Architecture, London 1970
– The Radiant City, New York 1964
Galbraith, John Kenneth: The Age of Uncertainty, Boston 1977
Geist, Johann Friedrich: Passagen. Ein Bautyp des 19. Jahrhunderts, München 1969
Giedion, Sigfried: Space Time and Architecture, Cambridge 1963
Goodman, Paul + Percival: Communitas, New York 1960
Gropius, Walter: The New Architecture and The Bauhaus, London 1935
Hamlin, Talbot: Architecture through the Ages, New York 1953
Hitchcock, Henry-Russell: The Pelican History of Art and Architecture Nineteenth and Twentieth Centuries, Baltimore 1969
– Johnson, Philip: The International Style, New York 1966
Howard, Ebenezer: Garden Cities of Tomorrow, London 1970
Jacobs, Jane: The Death and Life of Great American Cities, New York 1961
Jaynes, Julian: The Origins of Consciousness in the Breakdown of the Bicameral Mind, Boston 1976
Jencks, Charles: Le Corbusier and The Tragic View of Architecture, London 1973
– Modern Movements in Architecture, Garden City 1973
Joedicke, Jürgen: A History of Modern Architecture, London 1959
– Architecture Since 1945, London 1969
Kaufmann, Edgar Jr., Editor: The Rise of an American Architecture, New York 1970
Koestler, Arthur: The Ghost in the Machine, London 1967
Kuantes, P. W.: Transportation Aspects of Multi-use Centres, Oktober 1972
Newman, Oscar: CIAM '59 in Otterlo, Stuttgart 1961
Papper, Karl R.: The Open Society and Its Enemies, London 1945
Proshansky, Harold M., Ittleson, William H., Rivlin, Leanne G.: Environmental Psychology, New York 1967
Procos, Dimitri: Mixed Land Use: From Revival to Innovation, Stroudsburg 1976
Saalman, Howard: Medieval Cities, New York 1968
Sagan, Carl: The Dragons of Eden – Speculations on the Evolution of Human Intelligence, New York 1977
Sert, Josep Lluis: Le Corbusier. The Athens Charter, New York 1973
– Can Our Cities Survive?, Cambridge 1942
Smithson, Alison, Editor: Team 10 Primer, London 1968
Soleri, Paolo: Arcology: The City in the Image of Man, Cambridge 1969
Spelt, Jacob: Toronto, Don Mills 1972
Steegman, John: Victorian Taste – A Study of the Arts and Architecture from 1830 to 1876, Cambridge 1970
Wiebenson, Dora: Tony Garnier, The Cite Industrielle, New York 1969
Witherspoon, Robert E.: Mixed Use Developments, Washington 1976

Illustrations

Sources of Illustrations (Illustrations)

Part I

1 Seton, Müller, Martin: *Ancient Architecture. Mesopotamia, Egypt, Crete, Greece.*
Harry N. Abrams Inc., New York 1975
3 Saalman: *Haussmann, Paris, Transformed.*
George Braziller, New York 1971
5 Geist: *Passagen.*
Prestel, München 1969
8,9 Todd, Wheeler: *Utopia.*
Mansell Collection, London
10 Benevelo: *Origins of Modern Town Planning.*
Giuseppe Laterza & Figli, Roma
11 Ebenezer, Howard: *Garden Cities of to-Morrow.*
Reprinted by permission of Faber and Faber Ltd., London
12 Todd, Wheeler: *Utopia.*
Mansell Collection, London
13 Le Corbusier: *La Ville Radieuse.*
The Orion Press, New York 1933
18 Alison Smithson: *Team 10 Primer.*
Studio Vista, London, 1968
19,20 Architects: G. Candilis, A. Josic, S. Woods, M. Schiedhelm, Paris

Part III

1 *Die gute Einkehr*
4 Le Corbusier: Sonderausgabe.
Verlag für Architektur Artemis, Zürich
8 Zeidler Roberts Partnership
9 S. Giedion: *A Decade of new Architecture.*
Editions Girsberger, Zürich 1951
10,13 Zeidler Roberts Partnership
16 Institut für Grundlagen der modernen Architektur und Entwerfen.
Universität Stuttgart
17 T. Faegre: *Zelte. Die Architektur der Nomaden.*
Papyrus Verlag, Hamburg
26 Zeidler Roberts Partnership & A. Littlewood, Toronto
28,29 Zeidler Roberts Partnership, Toronto

35,36 Victor Gruen. *The Heart of our Cities.*
Simon & Schuster, New York 1964
39 Plan. Yorkdale Shopping Plaza
40,42 Zeidler Roberts Partnership, Toronto
43 Architectural Record, Oct. 1974
McGraw Hill Inc., New York
44 Architects: The Architects Collaborative, Cambridge, Mass.
45 Design Guidelines. City of Toronto Housing Dept. Zeidler Roberts Partnership, Toronto
49 Eberhard H. Zeidler, Toronto
51 Architectural Record, Oct. 1974
© 1974 by McGraw Hill Inc., New York
54 Zeidler Roberts Partnership, Toronto
55 Le Corbusier. *The Radiant City.*
The Orion Press, New York
56 Zeidler Roberts Partnership, Toronto
62 *Le Corbusier, P. Jeanneret. Oeuvre complète 1934–1938.*
Architectural Publishers Artemis, Zürich
63,64 P. Kwantes. *Traffic Quarterly, Oct 1972.* Eno Foundation
70 Insitut für Grundlagen der modernen Architektur und Entwerfen, Universität Stuttgart, Stuttgart
72 Zeidler Roberts Partnership, Toronto
77 Archives Photographiques, Paris
78 H. R. Hitchcook. *Early Victorian Architecture in Britain.* Yale University Press.
81 Ch. Moore. *Daniel H. Burnham, Architect.*
Da Capo Press Inc.
83 Benevelo: *Origins of Modern Town Planning.*
Guiseppe Laterza & Figli, Roma
85 *Architectural Design Vol. 49, 1979*
87 B. Fletcher. *A History of Architecture.*
The Athlone Press Ltd., 1961
88 R. Wittkower. *Architectural Principles.*
Academy Editions, London 1974

Index of Photographers

As far as can be ascertained the photographs were taken by the following photographers (pp., ills.):

Applied Photography Ltd. 101-8e
Bernard, Th. 99-7
Blessing, Hedrich 68-2
Brecht-Einzig Ltd. 41-6,7,8/61-6
Cravit, P. 128-50
Drummond, M. 21-7,8,9/121-31
Feddersen, H. P. 85-9
James, A. 82-10/141-66
Korab, B. 35-6,7/51-6,7,8,10
Lambert, S. 61-7,8
Louis & Partner 58-2/59-8
Martin, B. 35-5,6
Masson, F. 28-3/29-5,6
McGrath, Norman 53-8
Meyers, Barton 43-8
Obata, K. 35-4
Panda Ass. 23-6,7/102-19/115-28e
Payne, Chris 21-6
Rafelson, M. 87-7,9,10
von der Ropp, I. & A. 55-8
Rosenthal, St. 73-7/75-5,6,7
Rusz, M. 99-5/108-21,22/130-53
Rutter, H. 57-9
Samiy, Hamid 57-8
Samson, Ian 27-5,6/79-4,5/81-6/82-8,9/83-11/124-38
Stein, G. 145-75
Stient 89-5
Thompson, Ventulett & Stainback, Inc. 48-4
Wheeler, N. 52-2
Zeidler, E. H. 11-2/12-4,6,7/16-15,16/17-17/98-2,3/99-6/103-12/106-14,15/107-18/109-24/120-25/121-32/122-33/123-34/124-37/126-46/127-48/130-52/134-57,58/135-59/136-60,61/141-67/142-69/143-71/145-74,76/146-79/147-80/148-82/198-84/150-89/151-90,91,92/152-93,94/153-96
Zeidler, M. 103-11/140-65/142-68/144-73
Zeidler Roberts Partnership 101-8d/105-13f